# MAKING CUSHIONS

*OVER 30 DESIGNS TO*
*DECORATE YOUR HOME*

# MAKING CUSHIONS

## OVER 30 DESIGNS TO DECORATE YOUR HOME

### Linda Barker

Photography by Lizzie Orme

a Salamander book

Published by Salamander Books Limited
LONDON

A SALAMANDER BOOK

Published by Salamander Books Ltd,
129-137 York Way,
London N7 9LG,
United Kingdom

© Salamander Books Ltd, 1995

ISBN 0 86101 822 2

1 3 5 7 9 8 6 4 2

All correspondence concerning the content of this vol-
ume should be addressed to Salamander Books Ltd.

Author: Linda Barker
Project manager: Jane Donovan
Editor: Emma Callery
Design: Watermark Communications
Photographer: Lizzie Orme
Stylist: Linda Barker
Illustrations: Terry Evans
Film: Creative Text Ltd
Colour separation: P&W Graphics
Printed & bound in Great Britain by
Butler & Tanner Ltd, Frome and London

# Contents

# *Introduction*

Cushions are one of the easiest accessories to make for a room. They can add an essential finishing touch to the decor and they can be used in any room of the house. Cushions instantly add vitality, pattern and texture, and give a splash of colour to a sofa, chair or bed. Or use them to soften hard seating or to pad the arms of an old armchair. In a living room, for example, a sofa piled high with piped and tasselled cushions makes an inviting focal point and irresistible resting place. Cushions for your head, feet, even the small of your back, make reclining an art form. Who could resist such comfort? A chair placed near to a window, softened with feather cushions persuades you to come and sit down, relax and stay a while. Or a bright frog-shaped bean bag cushion on the nursery floor invites a small child to jump all over it.

Make cushion covers from fabric remnants and trimmings found in flea markets or antique sales. Whatever catches your eye, gather it up and squirrel it away - you never know when it may come in handy. In this book, the pearly buttons I found in a junk shop are used to decorate my lacy buttoned covers (see page 75) and are so much prettier displayed around the edge of a cushion cover than hidden away in a cupboard.

Only a couple of facts remain consistent throughout the book. First, all the fabrics you choose to use should be colourfast and pre-shrunk to avoid shrieks of horror when a floor cushion comes out of a washing machine in the guise of a marbled-effect scatter cushion. Second, check that fabrics can be easily cleaned. A dry-clean only fabric may look wonderful, but it's going to cost a fortune in cleaning bills every time a chocolate-sticky child chooses to use a treasured cushion as a hat, or as a cover to wrap peanut butter sandwiches inside.

With these exceptions, there are no hard and fast rules for choosing the right fabrics for cushions. For example, it is possible to use dress fabrics as well as heavy upholstery fabrics with equal success. Search out scraps of inexpensive fabrics for sewing appliqué panels and patchwork, or look for remnants of rich, extravagant fabrics with the knowledge that just half a metre isn't going to break the bank. In some of the projects that follow, I have displayed a piece of lace on a pretty gingham frilled cover, sewn scraps of fabrics to make charming appliqué designs and traditional patchwork, and even transformed a shrunken old sweater that may have otherwise have been thrown into the bin. I hope to encourage you to do the same.

# Materials and techniques

*Before tackling any of the cushions in this book it is well worth looking through this section as there are many techniques described that will make your cushion making so much more straightforward. In this way, the end result will be even more professional.*

## MATERIALS

A basic sewing kit should provide you with all the equipment you will need for the projects in this book. I keep all my bits and pieces together in a plastic tool kit which has handy compartments for tins, tape and threads. I try to always keep the following items in my sewing kit:

**Good scissors** Both a larger pair for cutting out and a small embroidery pair of scissors are indispensable for cushion-making. Pinking shears are useful, too, and may be a worthwhile investment if you intend to do lots of soft furnishings.

**Tailor's chalk** A supply of this for marking out fabric is preferable to pencil marks, and it is easily removed.

**Cloth tape and retractable steel tape** These are inexpensive items of equipment that I wouldn't be without.

**Graph paper** Needed for most patchwork designs.

**Steel dressmaking pins** These will not mark the fabric or leave holes. Occasionally, I use longer glass-headed pins, particularly for holding thicker fabrics together such as for quilting and appliqué.

**Needles** It is worth having these in assorted sizes, as well as darning needles and bodkins for threading work. Variously sized sewing machine needles are also necessary so that you can alter them according to the weight of fabric being sewn.

**Thread** My supply increases after each job as I am reluctant to discard even the smallest amount left on a reel. Generally, you should always use a thread that is compatible with the fabric you are working on. Strong threads for heavy canvas and denim-type fabric; lighter threads for muslin, organdie and silk. Choose natural threads for natural fabrics and, likewise, synthetic threads for synthetic fabrics.

**Zips** These should be of the correct weight and size for the cover fabric. Usually a 25cm/10in zip will be sufficient to allow most sizes of cushion pad into a cover, but smaller or larger ones can be used according to the size of cushion. I almost never use a metal zip as they do not wash as well as the plastic ones, nor are they as discreet.

**Miscellaneous items** Other useful things to keep at hand are packs of neutral-coloured bias binding, wadding and self-cover buttons of all sizes. A well-used item in my tool kit is a plastic seam ripper, designed for unpicking seams and stitches.

### GLOSSARY OF FABRICS

This list includes all the fabrics I have used in this book, and a few that I haven't used, but I feel would be suitable. Remember, that by adding unusual bits and pieces you personalize your covers.

**Calico** A woven cotton fabric, lighter than canvas. It is usually sold in its natural colourway, but it may be bleached white or dyed.

**Canvas** (also referred to as cotton duck) A strong fabric, sometimes woven from linen and occasionally from synthetic fibres. It comes in a variety of weights: a lightweight canvas is most suitable for cushion making.

**Chintz** A cotton fabric that is either printed or plain and has a characteristic glaze finish.

**Damask** A self-patterned traditional fabric made from cotton, linen or silk on a traditional jacquard loom. It is often used for table covers and napkins.

**Denim** Characteristically used for blue jeans, but can be purchased off-the-roll for upholstery and covers.

**Felt** A fabric made from matted fibres that are pounded, shrunk and bonded together to make a soft fabric that does not fray when cut.

**Gingham** A traditionally woven, checked fabric. Usually cotton or mixed cotton and synthetic fibres.

**Hessian** A very strong, coarse weave fabric made from jute or hemp.

**Lace** A delicate, fine, openweave fabric created by knotting or twisting the threads to form a pattern. It is usually white or cream.

**Linen** A strong cloth woven from flax fibres. It is prone to shrinkage and creasing if it is not mixed with another fibre. Wash the cloth prior to sewing to pre-shrink the fibres.

**Muslin** A very soft, light fabric, woven quite loosely, making it semi-transparent.

**Organdie** A finely woven, thin fabric that is semi-transparent and stiff.

**Provençal print** A traditional French country print fabric with brightly coloured, small-scale motifs and floral patterns.

**Raw silk** (sometimes known as wild silk) A natural fibre that is spun and then woven into soft fabric with a slubby coarse texture.

**Silk dupion** A slubby, textured silk, but is now often made from other fibres.

**Tapestry** A heavy, woven fabric, often showing a traditional pictorial design.

**Tartan** A traditionally woven fabric in two or more colours creating a checked cloth. Individual designs relate to specific Scottish families or clans.

**Ticking** A heavy cotton, twill fabric used for pillows, mattresses and bolsters. Traditionally woven with a fine stripe in black, blue or red.

**Toile de Jouy** A traditional cotton print in one colour (usually red, blue or sepia) on a natural or off-white ground. The designs often depict rural scenes and rustic figures.

**Velvet** A soft, luxurious warp pile fabric with a dense, short pile.

**Wadding** A soft and fibrous cotton or polyester padding which is available in several weights. It is used for quilting.

### USING THE TEMPLATES AT THE BACK OF THE BOOK

On pages 90-94 are a series of templates designed to be used with the cushions in this book. Either photocopy them as they are or enlarge to an appropriate size and then cut out the template.

If you don't have a photocopier to hand, trace the designs and transfer onto paper by drawing over the back of the tracing with a soft pencil and then going over the front again; or enlarge them using the grid method. To do this, draw a grid of squares over the relevant template in the book and draw a correspondingly larger grid on your sheet of paper. Copying the outline square by square, reproduce the design.

Draw a regular grid over the outline.

Scale up the drawing by enlarging the outline onto a larger grid.

## CLOSINGS

Whether your cushion is closed with a zip or an envelope fastening or a simple tied fastening, always decide on the method closing before purchasing or cutting out the fabric. Each closing will require a different amount of fabric. If you are in any doubt, cut the cushion pieces from paper before you begin and lay these onto a flat surface to determine the amount of fabric you will need.

Occasionally the best option for closing a cushion is to simply stitch the opening closed. For the projects in this book where I feel this is necessary I have included this making up in the relevant text.

Leave a small gap for turning the cushion through to the right side.

### ENVELOPE CASING

This is perhaps the simplest fastening. Cut the required square of rectangle for the front of the cushion cover including 2.5cm/1in seam allowances. Cut out a second piece for the back of the cover the width of which is the same as the first piece, but the length should be one-and-three-quarters the length of the front. Cut this piece in half across its length. Turn the raw edges under along each side of the horizontal cut.

Lay these two pieces over the cushion front with right sides together and raw edges even. Stitch around the sides and turn the cover to the right side through the opening.

For a button-backed closing, sew buttonholes and buttons onto the two parts of the vent prior to stitching the front to the back.

Take the tiniest stitch for an almost invisible join.

### INSERTING A ZIP

There are two options for inserting a zip. The first is to insert it along the outside seam, or to insert it across the centre back of the cushion. With the exception of shaped cushions, the choice is yours. Here it is recommended that you insert a zip across the centre of the back to avoid fitting a zip around curves which can look bulky and untidy.

**Fitting a zip in the seam** Cut the front and back parts of the cover, including the seam allowances. Place these with right sides facing and keeping the raw edges even. Place the zip centrally along the edge of the seam and mark the ends of the zip using tailor's chalk.

Sew the ends of the seam up to the chalk marks. Then tack the seam where the zip is to be stitched. Press the seam open and lay the zip wrong side up along the tacked seam. Sew it into place using the zipper foot on your sewing machine. Undo the tacking and open the zip. Stitch around the other edges keeping the right sides of the fabric together and the raw edges even. Turn the cover to the right side, through the zip.

Tack the seam by hand so the stitches can easily be removed.

Press the seam open and sew the zip over the allowance.

Remove the tacking stitches and open the zip.

**Fitting a zip across the back of the fabric** Cut the front of the cushion cover as before and cut another piece to the same size plus a further 5cm/2in to the width. Fold this piece of fabric in half and cut across the centre. Lay these two halves together with right sides facing and raw edges even and mark the central position of the zip using tailor's chalk. Continue as for fitting a zip in the seam (above) first sewing the ends of the seam up to the chalk marks.

### TIED CLOSINGS

Another closing option is to fasten a cushion with fabric or ribbon ties. The simplest way to do this is to leave one side unstitched and then sew the ties on the front and back. On larger cushions it is advisable to include a flap inside the closing edge to stop the cushion pushing out around the ties (rather like a pillow flap). To do this, make the front slightly longer than the back. Seam one of the short edges and fold to the back until the length of the front is the same as the back. Stitch front to back with right sides facing, as usual.

Alternatively, ties can be sewn at both sides of the envelope casing (see above) on the reverse of the cushion, to be tied neatly at the back.

The flap holds the pad inside the cushion like a pillow flap.

## MAKING SHAPED CUSHIONS

Shapes and sizes of cushions are limitless, ranging from tiny rectangles that support your neck to huge floor cushions that may provide an answer to a seating problem. Square, round, hexagonal, even star-shaped - the choice is up to you. Armed with a paper template you could make just about any shape of cushion you could imagine.

### SHAPING TO FIT A CHAIR SEAT

To shape a cover to fit a chair seat, simply lay a sheet of brown paper or newspaper over the seat and mark around the perimeter with a pencil. Cut out the template and fold it in half to check that it is symmetrical and then lay this onto your fabric and pin in place. The best filling for this type of squab cushion is foam, providing a flattish cushion with a firm support.

Lay the paper directly onto the seat and draw the outline.

If you're making a squab cushion or a closed fastening, cut the shape from a double layer of fabric.

### MAKING A HEART-SHAPED COVER

First fold a sheet of brown paper or newspaper in half, and then draw half of a heart shape onto the paper, or use one of the heart-shaped templates on page 90. Use the fold line as the centre of the heart and cut it out from the double thickness of paper. Unfold to reveal the whole, perfectly symmetrical heart-shaped template. Pin this directly onto your fabric and cut out the front and back of the cushion bearing in mind which type of closing you need (see pages 12-13). If you want to put a zip into the middle of the back see page 36 for cutting and sewing.

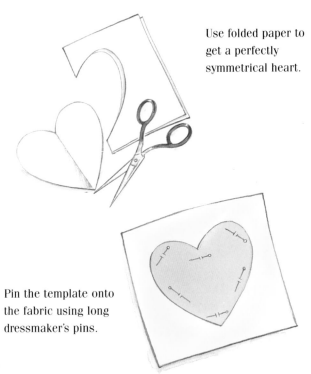

Use folded paper to get a perfectly symmetrical heart.

Pin the template onto the fabric using long dressmaker's pins.

### MORE COMPLICATED SHAPES OF CUSHION COVER

For a shaped cushion that is more complicated in design, such as the daisy-shaped seat pad on page 36, break down the separate components used to make up the design. In this case, the seat pad is simply a round centre and you can use a dinner plate to make the circular outline. For the petal template, the base of a tumbler is ideal, but remember to extend both lines from the edges of the glass downwards to square the ends of the petals prior to sewing.

A dinner plate makes an ideal guide to draw around.

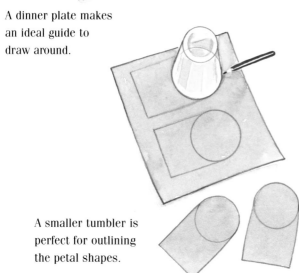

A smaller tumbler is perfect for outlining the petal shapes.

Use a flexible cloth tape for accurate measuring.

Mark off the measurement using tailor's chalk.

### CUSHION PADS AND FILLINGS

Use a cushion pad with either a feather or a down filling, or a pad with a mixture of both. Plastic or latex foam chips are less expensive, but these tend to compact and go lumpy after a time and need to be replaced.

Some of the cushions in this book are filled with foam cut to size with a pair of sharp scissors. For deeper cushions, such as the damask piped squab on page 49, either fill with a deep piece of foam, or insert two thinner layers.

Always use fillings and cushion pads with the relevant safety standards. This information is always supplied with those products that have been fully checked.

### MEASURING A BOLSTER CUSHION PAD

Bolster cushion covers are shaped to cover the size of the pad. For a bolster that has both ends gathered, you need to cut a rectangle of your chosen fabric the width of which is equal to the circumference of the bolster plus a 5cm/2in seam allowance. The length needs to be the same as the bolster plus the radius of each end and a 2.5cm/1in seam allowance for each end.

### MAKING YOUR OWN CUSHION PAD

For shaped cushions you will often have to make your own cushion pad. Use the same template as for the cushion and cut two pieces of muslin or calico to a size slightly larger all around. With right sides facing, sew the front and back together leaving a small gap. Turn the right side out, stuff with loose filling and sew the gap closed. Use this as a pad for the cushion.

## EDGINGS

Edgings can make all the difference to a cushion and there are many types to choose from. Ready-made trimmings are easily available and can either be stitched around the edge of an existing cushion cover or be sewn between the top and bottom pieces of a new cover. Whichever method you choose, they are quite straightforward to apply.

### SEWING ON TRIMMINGS

Measure all around the edge of the cushion cover and add on an extra 5cm/2in to the measurement for joining. Hand sew the trimming to the edge of the cover using strong thread and tiny stitches. Make a small hole in the seam with a seam ripper and tuck the ends of the trimming inside the cushion cover.

Hand sew a fringed edging around the edge of a cushion.

### STITCHING TRIMMINGS AND FRILLS

Lay the trimming or frill along the edge of the right side of the top of the cushion cover with the fringing or frill towards the centre of the cushion. Align the heading tape or fabric edge with the raw edge of the cushion. Pin the trimming and then stitch around the four sides, keeping an even seam allowance.

Use tiny hand stitches using a thread that matches the edging.

Sew a frilled edge between the top and bottom pieces, keeping raw edges even.

### ATTACHING DECORATIVE CORDS

To stitch on a decorative cord, use a strong thread in a complementary colour and use tiny stitches to sew this along the edges of the cover. To join the cord, unravel the ends slightly and then twist the cords together. Oversew the ends to neaten and prevent the threads from unravelling around the cord.

## PIPING

If you have difficulty finding a trimming to match your cushion, make your own piping cord. Mark out 5cm/2in-wide strips across the diagonal (bias) of your fabric using tailor's chalk and a long tape measure. Cut the resulting strips from the fabric.

Open up the small seam and press.

Cut the bias strips across the grain of fabric.

Join the strips together across the grain, pinning the strips together with right sides facing and at right angles to each other. Sew together, trim and then press the seam open at the back. Fold the bias strip around the piping cord with the right side uppermost and aligning the raw edges. Use the zipper foot on your sewing machine to stitch as close to the edge of the cord as possible. Always use the zipper foot as this will allow you to stitch close to the cord. If the regular sewing foot is used, you may find that the casing will start to pucker.

Pin the piping along the edges of the right side of the top of the cushion cover, keeping the raw edges even. To fit it around the cushion corners, snip into the piping's seam allowance. Pin and then stitch in place.

To join the corded piping, do not sew the two ends onto the fabric. Instead, unpick the stitches from one end of the piping and fold the fabric back. Cut the cords to butt up together and fold the fabric back over the cord. Fold under the raw edge and enclose the piping cord. Hand sew in place.

## SAFETY NOTE

Care should be taken when sewing on trimmings, beads and buttons as you might find that babies and small children could pull these off if they are not very firmly stitched in place.

If you are making cushions for the nursery or for very small children and babies, it is best to avoid making cushions that are decorated in this way.

Care should also be given when purchasing cushion pads and fillings, making sure these are protected with the appropriate safety standards.

## EMBROIDERY STITCHES

Often a little hand stitching is used to embellish the detailing on the front of a cushion cover. Also, occasionally, hand stitches are better than those produced on the sewing machine for performing certain tasks such as a double line of running stitches for gathering long frills.

### RUNNING STITCH

Small neat stitches of equal length are stitched on the front and back of the fabric. When stitching a line of tacking, if inserting a zip for example, use this stitch, but with longer stitches on the right side and smaller ones behind. It is often better to use a contrasting thread which is easily seen for removal once the main stitching is finished.

An ideal stitch for setting in a zip.

### DOUBLE RUNNING STITCH

Work evenly-spaced stitches across two rows, a short distance apart. Leave the threads loose at one end and slide the fabric along the threads, gathering the folds evenly. Fasten off the loose ends.

Try to keep the stitches regular and even.

Pull the two threads together to draw up the fabric.

### BACK STITCH

This is a short stitch which is strong enough to hold seams if necessary. Sew one stitch and come through the top fabric with the needle as if to start another stitch. Take the needle backwards and insert it at the end of the previous stitch bringing the needle back up an equal stitch length in front. Repeat to finish a line of stitches. Three back stitches sewn on top of each other are often used to finish threads.

Vary the lengths of the stitches depending on the look you want, but keep their length even.

### LADDER STITCH

Use this stitch when sewing appliqué designs onto the right side of fabric where a neat, discreet stitch is needed. An oversized version of this is used in a decorative way around the canvas panel on the stencilled pig cushion (see page 81).

Working on the right side of the fabric, knot the thread and insert the needle from the back to the right side. Take a stitch exactly opposite the point where the needle has come out, pass the needle underneath and then bring it out as before, only a little further along the seam. Progress as before.

For a line of invisible stitches, use a thread that matches the face of the fabric. However, sometimes - as in appliqué - you may wish to sew an overstated stitch in which case you should use three strands of a coloured embroidery thread and a larger stitch. Regardless of the length of the stitch, always keep the stitches even and follow a regular spacing between each stitch.

### CROSS STITCH

Use three strands of embroidery thread to sew this stitch. Knot the thread and bring the needle up from underneath the work. Stitch down into the diagonal corner, bringing the needle down through the work and then upwards to a point directly opposite where the needle had first come out. Move the needle across to the opposite diagonal and through to the underside, creating the characteristic cross.

Repeat the procedure to complete the stitches, remembering that half stitches may be formed around the outside of a shape if required.

This understated stitch that we probably all learnt at infant school, is elegant when used as decorative detailing on the cover of a cushion. Use the classic combination such as blue on white fabric for an attractive finish.

Once several stitches
have been formed,
you will find it easier
to build up a regular
pattern of stitches.

Use tiny stitches for
an invisible seam.

## QUILTING

Quilting has traditional roots and yet its application can be both modern and traditional. The technique outlined here is stitched on a sewing machine and is simpler in comparison to the hand-quilted fabrics so often seen in museums and magazines and takes up only a fraction of the time to produce.

1 Place a layer of wadding between two fabric pieces to create a sandwich effect with the main fabric uppermost. Tack around the edges and pin across the centre with long, glass-headed pins.

2 If your main fabric has an outline to follow, such as the fruit and flower urn on the cushion on page 27, then follow this with the line of stitches.

3 When you are machine quilting, it is easier to work the lines of stitching between an embroidery hoop as this keeps the fabric taut at all times. Work from the middle of the work out. In order to slide the double hoop underneath the sewing foot you may need to remove part of the foot, but once the hoop is in place, fit the foot back onto the sewing machine. Remove the pins from the area to be quilted within the hoop.

4 Drop the feeder teeth on the sewing machine so that you can guide the fabric underneath the sewing foot wherever you wish to go. Twists and turns in the direction of sewing are easier to do when the teeth are retracted.

5 To establish the flow of stitches and as there are no teeth to pull the fabric through, move the embroidery hoop to feed the fabric under the sewing foot. It may take a little while to get used to this technique at first, but keep practising and you will get there. It is best to work on a piece of scrap fabric before committing to the real thing. Follow the outline printed on the fabric and feed the fabric under the needle as if you were drawing with it.

Pin all the fabrics in place before sewing.

6 Once enough of the design has been stitched, remove the hoops and the remaining pins (if there are any) and tidy up the work. There will be many small threads to snip off and the fabric can then be used to make up a cushion cover.

If you start to use the sewing machine continuously, say for four or five minutes, at any one time, you will need to rest the motor. Do this by stopping sewing for approximately two minutes for every five minutes sewing on the machine.

Quilting can also be sewn with straight lines in the more traditional manner of squares or diamonds. If you wish, you could use this more regular form of machine quilting as an introduction to the freestyle method of quilting

If you use the ready-quilted wadding, you will already have a regular grid which will form a guide for your stitch lines. Pin the top fabric underneath the wadding with long dressmaker's pins and then carefully sew over the stitching lines. Turn the fabric over to reveal the right side.

## APPLIQUÉ

One of the delights about working in appliqué is that all the materials are found in bags of scrap fabrics and that basically you are stitching something from practically nothing at all. With a small piece of fabric here, and a larger piece there, you can easily create great images.

1 Separate your fabrics into patterns and plains, textures and colours. Some fabrics are easier to work with than others. For example, velvet will fray until it disintegrates into practically nothing, whereas felt does not fray at all and because of this quality it is perfect for appliqué. That is not to say that I never use velvet for this type of sewing - the combination of many fabrics makes for an interesting match.

2 If using fabrics that are susceptible to fraying, if at all possible oversew the raw edges with a sewing machine using zigzag stitch (see the appliqué hearts cushion on page 34). However, some pieces will be so small that this is not possible as it is so fiddly so it is best to avoid them altogether.

3 Once you have decided upon your design and which fabrics are going where, cut out the individual pieces remembering to add a small allowance all around for turning under. Carefully press under the turnings and stitch in place.

4 Arrange the fabric pieces on the background cloth, pin and then sew in place using tiny, invisible stitching. Turn under raw edges whenever possible to avoid the fabric fraying.

5 Embroidery stitches can then be applied over the appliqué, adding decorative detailing. Experiment with different stitches as you go along, filling in parts of the design or simply adding small details. Beads and sequins can also add to the overall effect of the appliqué. Sew these on very securely, using a strong thread.

A pea pod is a very simple outline for appliqué.

Appliqué can be inspired by many things, even something as simple and commonplace as this pea pod or the carrot that appears on page 38. It may be that you have a particularly beautiful piece of fabric that inspires the design or something you have seen in a shop, museum or gallery.

Books and magazines can be equally wonderful sources for reference. If you don't have the space to store old magazines then tear out pages that interest you and keep these together in a large manilla envelope or two. It is amazing how looking back through these old collections can often spark off new and innovative ideas.

Also get into the habit of saving every scrap of fabric - tiny scraps can be stored in jam jars, and larger pieces neatly popped into bags or shoe boxes. Sort the fabrics by colour and if the collections become too big, then sort them out yet further, this time by texture and pattern.

## PATCHWORK

Patchwork must be one of the oldest country crafts and whereas a quilt can sometimes take years to complete, a patchwork cushion will only take up a fraction of that time.

1 Work out your design on a piece of graph paper. You could use a traditional design like the Ohio star used for the patchwork cushion on page 51 or make up your own design. Whichever you choose, draw it carefully onto the graph paper.

2 Cut the pieces from the paper using a pair of sharp scissors following the lines diligently. To help with your piecing later on, mark which shapes join together on the back of each piece of paper.

Pin and cut each template before sewing together.

3 To make stronger templates, use stiff cardboard instead of graph paper and use the resulting shapes as master templates. This is particularly useful if the same shape is to be used again and again. Place the cardboard templates onto rough paper and draw around them to make as many paper shapes as are required, and then cut them out.

4 Choose a selection of fabrics that work well together. Plain fabrics will offset patterned ones, and dark colours will project paler ones. By assembling the groups of fabrics you will be able to assess what each of them will do.

5 Pin the templates onto the wrong side of the fabrics and cut out each piece, adding a small seam allowance on each side. Turn the allowance over to the back of the template and tack. Continue this until all the templates have been tacked.

6 Stitch together patchwork pieces. Start in the centre of each design and work your way outwards. To stitch pieces together, place with right sides facing and hand sew the two parts together using tiny overstitches. Continue to make up the patchwork in this way. Do not remove the paper until each square, or part of a design, is complete.

7 The patchwork cushion featured on page 51 uses four such stars. Should you become addicted to the whole process, continue making the Ohio stars until the patchwork becomes a bedcover.

8 If the process is becoming laboured then sew two stars and two plain squares together - positioning them diagonally - to make up the front of the cushion cover. Or easier still, sew one single Ohio star for the centre of the cushion and then border this with plain fabric pieces. With ideas like this you will find that it is very easy to adapt the patchwork to suit your own requirements.

## STENCILLING

Stencilling is addictive - so be warned. The little pig featured on the stencilled cushion on page 81 will be almost guaranteed to turn up on bedroom walls, pillowcases, quilt covers, and the rest. But who could resist it?

Cutting stencils is easy once you have the right equipment to hand. A sharp craft knife and some stencil card and a cutting surface is all you require.

1 Either use the pig outline on page 90 or design your own stencil and draw the outline onto the stencil card.

2 Fix the card to the cutting board and cut out the outline using the sharp craft knife. Always cut away from your supporting hand and turn the craft board as you move around corners.

3 Fix the stencil onto the surface to be decorated fixing it with double-sided tape.

4 Use fabric paint and stencil the design by dipping a slightly damp stencil brush into the paint. Dab off the excess onto a piece of scrap paper or kitchen towel and transfer the paint through the stencil. Use a tapping motion with the brush.

5 In larger areas, vary the pressure used on the brush to provide lighter and darker shaded patches. This will give more interest to the overall design.

6 Leave the fabric paint to dry thoroughly and fix the paint according to the manufacturer's instructions. Usually it is set with a hot iron smoothed over the reverse side of the fabric.

7 Remove the stencil and position elsewhere if repeating it for another cushion. Check the back of the stencil before repositioning to ensure no paint has dripped onto the reverse of the design.

Use specially formulated fabric paints when stencilling onto cloth.

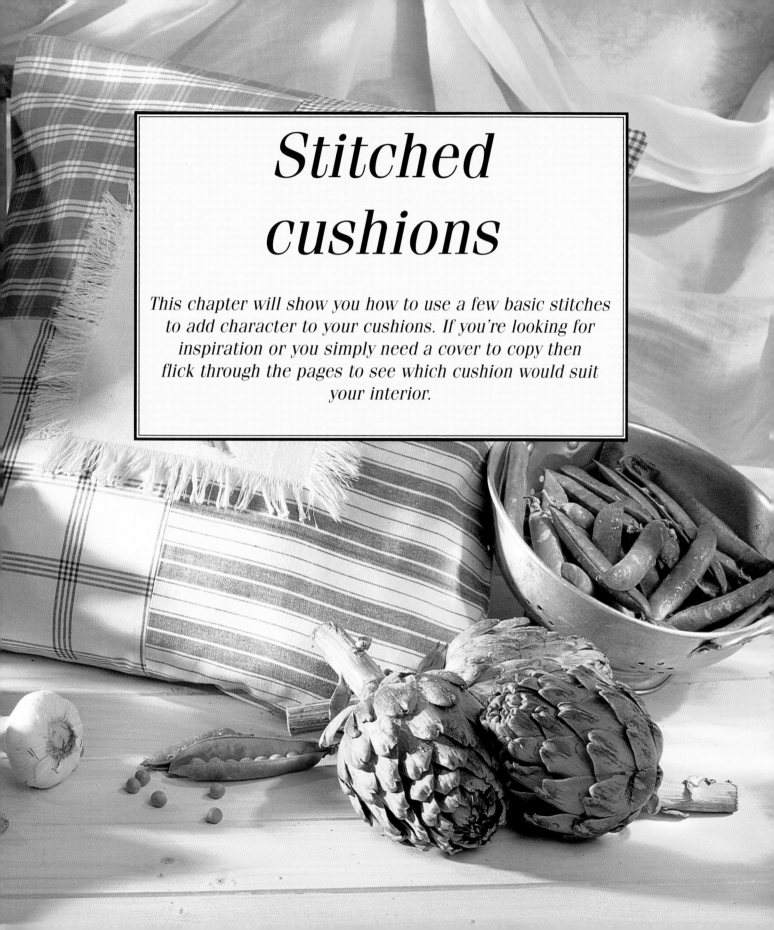

# Stitched cushions

This chapter will show you how to use a few basic stitches to add character to your cushions. If you're looking for inspiration or you simply need a cover to copy then flick through the pages to see which cushion would suit your interior.

# Quilted cushion

Most fabrics are suitable for quilting, but a material with a pattern such as this flower and fruit urn provides a really obvious outline to follow when stitching. So this type of fabric may be the best kind to look out for if you are quilting for the first time. The quilted appearance occurs because of the layer of wadding sandwiched between the face and base fabrics. As the line of stitches progresses around the outline, the quilting becomes more noticeable. This method of quilting is done on the sewing machine (see page 20) but traditionally quilting was done by hand and involved many hours of dedication and diligence.

Cut the face fabric to the required size and place this over a similar sized piece of wadding which in turn is placed over a cotton backing cloth. Use long pins to secure the three layers together and then machine quilt the design on the fabric as outlined on page 20. Follow the outlines of the printed design and aim to keep the stitches regular and as even as possible.

As one area is stitched, release the embroidery hoop and pull an unworked area through the hoop. Remove the pins from this area, squeeze together the hoops and continue as before. Carefully work as little or as much of the design as you wish, continuously checking the effect as you progress.

Cut the fabric pieces for the back of the cushion taking into account your preferred method of closing (see pages 12-13). Then sew the front and back parts of the cushion together, with right sides facing and raw edges even. Turn the right side out and fill with an appropriate cushion pad (see page 15).

If you prefer to do some freestyle quilting, sandwich a layer of wadding between two pieces of plain fabric and pin together as above. Then lightly draw your design onto the fabric with tailor's chalk and follow these lines when stitching. Look at antique quilts in museums or contemporary pictures in books to seek inspiration.

*Left* Place the face fabric over the wadding which in turn is placed over the base fabric. Use long pins to hold together.

*Right* Sew around the outlines of the printed motif, stitching as little or as much of the design as you wish.

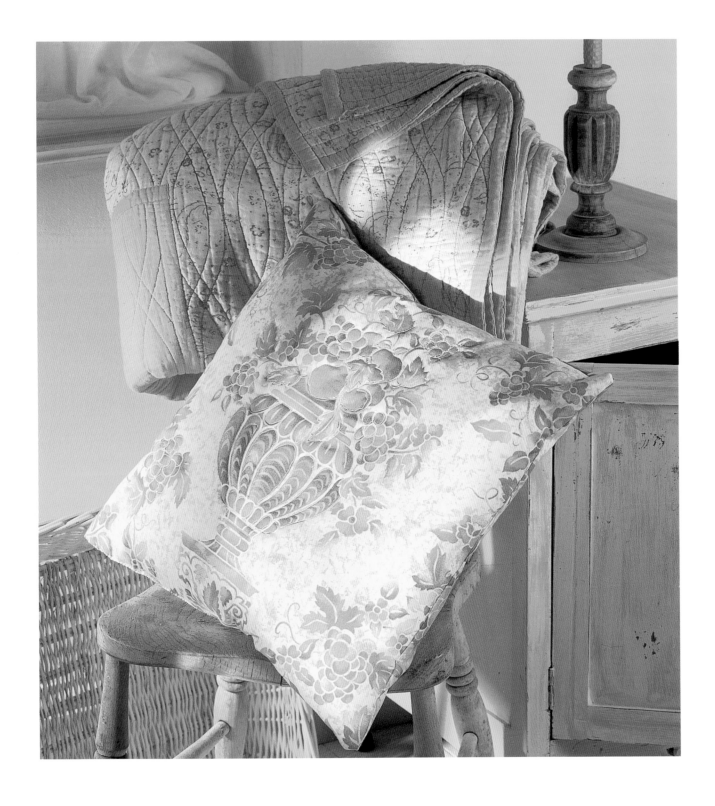

# Beaded heart cushion

For this cushion, stitch two fringed pieces of canvas diagonally opposite each other on the front of the cushion cover and decorate the other corners with pretty calico hearts that are first crossed with thin ribbon and then decorated with tiny beads.

Natural colours are very restful and here I have used toning calico and canvas in addition to the natural cotton ribbon. As both the fringed canvas and the beaded hearts are stitched onto the top of the cushion, first prepare the cover. Cut the fabric pieces for the front and back of the cushion taking into account your preferred method of closing (see pages 12-13). Set the back fabric aside.

Fold the front into quarters and press lightly with a warm iron to mark them clearly. Cut two pieces of canvas to fit neatly into two diagonally opposite corners and carefully cut these to exactly this size, less 2.5cm/1in all around.

Fringe the four edges of each piece of canvas by teasing out the fibres to create a 2.5cm/1in fringe. Pin and then sew each piece of canvas onto the cover, keeping the stitching line close to the inside edge of the fringing.

Enlarge the larger heart template on page 90 on a photocopier to an appropriate size or transfer it onto paper (see page 11). Use the template to cut out two calico hearts and then cut strips of thin cotton ribbon to make a chequerboard pattern over the surface of the heart. Pin the ends of the ribbon in place to hold them prior to sewing.

Once the ribbons are stitched, trim them up to the edge of the hearts and then pin each heart in place on the front of the cover. Use a close zigzag stitch on your sewing machine to sew around the outside edge. Finally, sew each tiny bead onto the heart at the points where the ribbons cross.

Sew the front and back parts of the cushion together, with right sides facing and raw edges even. Turn the cover to the right side and fill with an appropriate cushion pad (see page 15).

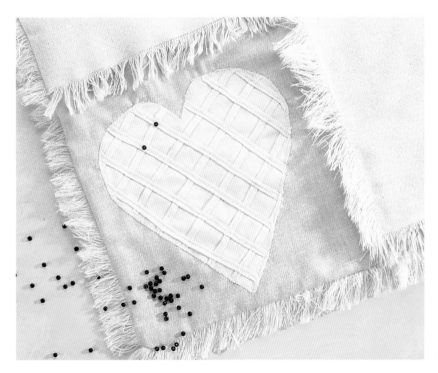

*Left* Small beads are used for practical reasons more than any other; it would be uncomfortable to rest your head against beads that are any larger than these.

*Right* The natural colours of this cushion emphasize the beadwork.

# Blue cross stitch bolster

Bolster cushions are extremely comfortable for supporting the neck, either on a bed or on a sofa. The ends of this cushion are simply gathered and trimmed with a ribbon, stitched neatly over the gathering stitches. As an alternative, cover a large button with the same fabric as used for the blue and white fabric trimming and stitch these over the ends.

Cut a rectangle from an appropriate fabric following the measurement instructions given on page 15. Sew three evenly spaced, 2.5cm/1in-wide strips of blue and white fabric across the rectangle to run around the bolster. To cover the raw edges, sew a strip of lace over each edge. If your lace has a line of threads forming a channel, such as the one I have used here, thread a narrow ribbon through the threads and tie with a small bow at the front for a pretty detailing.

Sew the long ends of the bolster together, aligning the lace strips and with right sides facing and raw edges even. Press the seam allowance open and turn to the right side. Turn under the seam allowance at each end and stitch, and then run a line of gathering stitches close to the machine stitching using a strong thread.

Slide the bolster cushion pad inside the cover, leaving an equal amount of fabric at either end. Pull up the gathering threads at each end and stitch these closed to fasten the ends of the bolster. Tie with a decorative ribbon if required, or stitch on a covered button over the gathers.

Draw a heart and a diamond shape onto the front of the bolster in the gaps between the three strips and work cross stitch into these shapes (see page 19). If your bolster cover fabric does not have a square weave to follow, it may be easier to cross stitch the heart and diamond motifs onto a piece of Aida canvas (specifically made for embroidery work) as this will produce an even cross-stitch pattern which can be sewn directly onto the cushion cover.

*Right* Perfect for supporting the head, this bolster cushion would be just right on a sofa or bed.

# Embroidery squares

For this cushion, tiny squares of translucent organza are stitched over silk flower petals. Each square is then decoratively stitched using pale embroidery thread, resulting in a delicate pattern that is strikingly beautiful. I chose a loose weave hessian fabric for the background as its rough texture contrasts perfectly with the fine organza.

Cut a hessian square to the required size of the finished cushion, plus 2.5cm/1in all around for turnings. Press the fabric carefully, taking care not to twist the weave in any direction. Lay the fabric onto a flat surface and smooth down.

Strip a silk flower head for its petals making sure all the plastic parts are removed from the flowers. Press each flower carefully using a warm iron and a damp cloth. Position the flowers over the surface of the hessian following a regular pattern (see below), but do not pin them yet.

Cut 5cm/2in squares from the organza using pinking shears. If you do not have these, brush a little white glue (PVA) around the cut edges of each small square to prevent fraying the edges.

Place each organza square directly over each flower head. Holding the centre lightly with a finger, with your other hand move the flowers slightly from underneath the organza so some of the petals project beyond the edges. Vary the extent of the projection for each flower and from which side of the square they project. Pin the squares and silk flowers onto the hessian.

To create the hand-stitched spiral coils, use two strands of embroidery thread and a simple backstitch. Lightly draw the coils with a piece of tailor's chalk before stitching. Make sure that some of the stitches trap the petals underneath to secure the flowers to the hessian.

Once the decoration is stitched, iron the fabric once again. Select a straight stitch on your sewing machine and sew around the edges of each organza square to keep the squares flat and prevent fraying. Stitch the hessian over a cotton fabric and trim to the same size. Then stitch this and a backing fabric together taking into account your preferred method of closing (see pages 12-13). Fill with an appropriate cushion pad (see page 15).

*Left* Once the position of the silk flowers is determined, pin each organza square onto the hessian.

*Right* The delicate flowers and translucent organza are perfect contrasts against the hessian weave. This cushion measures 43cm/17in square, but you could make one to suit your own requirements.

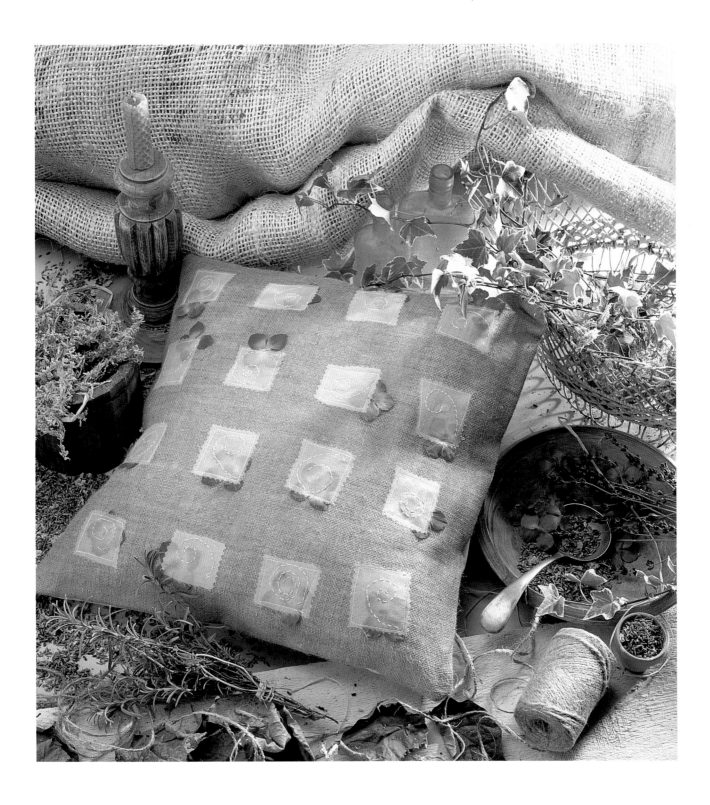

# Appliqué hearts cushion

Each square on this attractive cushion has been decorated with a heart motif using scraps of different fabrics. Each square of linen with its appliqué heart is then embellished with colourful embroidery thread and tiny beads. The effect is wonderful, and yet it really is gloriously easy to do.

The beauty of this technique is that you can use many different textures and colours of fabric, which all combine to create a rich effect. Choose from inexpensive gingham and felt, linen and printed cotton, as well as more luxurious velvet and silks. A plain fabric is best for the background squares so that the colourful hearts are really pronounced.

Assemble all your scraps and decide which combinations work well together. Then enlarge the heart templates (you will need a small and a large heart for each square) on page 90 on a photocopier to appropriate sizes or transfer them onto paper (see page 11). Using these templates, cut out the hearts. Cut the squares according to the size of cushion you require. As a guide, I found that 15cm/6in squares were an ideal

size, but you could make smaller or larger versions of this cushion, depending on your own requirements, or simply increase or reduce the number of squares. You may also find it useful to cut a paper template for the squares. It is surprising how quickly squares can become distorted when you start to use fabric pieces as templates.

Pin a small heart over a larger one. Then use three strands of coloured embroidery thread and a bold overstated ladder stitch (see page 19) to secure the hearts together. Sew tiny beads over the surface of the inner heart. When you are happy with the appliqué effect, pin the hearts centrally over each linen square and sew them carefully in place using the zigzag stitch on your sewing machine.

Choose a coordinating fabric to back the cushion and cut it out taking into account your preferred method of closing (see pages 10-11). Sew a muslin casing for the pad (see page 15) and insert it in the cushion cover. As a final embellishment, sew tiny tassels around the edges of the cushion.

*Left* Appliqué hearts are stitched with coloured embroidery thread and tiny beads for decorative effect. Use buttons or sequins if you prefer; look out for strands of costume jewellery in junk shops that are often sold for next to nothing.

*Right* The finished cushion is composed from a variety of fabric scraps combined to create a unique decoration. I used a natural linen, but cheaper canvas or cotton would be just as effective.

# Daisy-shaped seat pad

Shaped cushions can make a plain chair look interesting and provided you are careful when cutting the template, even a complicated shape such as this daisy can be stitched without a problem. See pages 14-15 for information on making shaped cushions.

Use a plate as a guide to make the paper template for the front of the cushion, and then cut out a circle of fabric. Cut the template in half, separate the two by 5cm/2in and secure with sticky tape. Use this new shape to cut out the back of the cushion. Cut the resulting fabric piece in half and then tack the seam where the zip is inserted and sew the remainder of the seam closed. Lay the zip wrong side up along the tacking stitches and sew in place using the zipper foot. Undo the tacking and open the zip.

For the petal templates see page 15. Cut out the template and use it to cut enough petals from a double thickness of fabric (folded with right sides facing) to go around the flower. Sew an even allowance around the curved part of each petal and notch the curves using a sharp pair of scissors to ease turning. Turn through and press the seams.

Place the petals around the cushion front with right sides facing. The base of the petals should touch slightly where the stitching line is to be and the raw edges will overhang slightly. Move the petals around until they are placed correctly and stitch in place.

Cut simple flower shapes from linen fabric backed with fusible webbing and fix onto the cushion front with a warm iron. Also on the front of the cushion and using the sewing machine, sew coils of stitches by dropping the feeder teeth and turning the fabric under the sewing foot as you work.

Sew the front and back parts of the cushion together, with right sides facing and raw edges even, and following the previous line of stitches. Turn to the right sides, press and fill with a piece of thin foam cut to the same size.

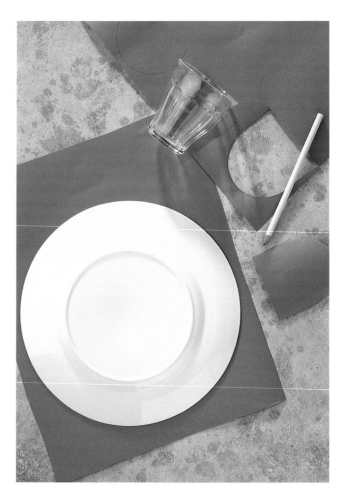

*Above* Draw around a plate and a glass to make outlines for the paper templates.

*Right* Fill the daisy cover with a piece of foam cut to size so that it lies flat on the chair seat.

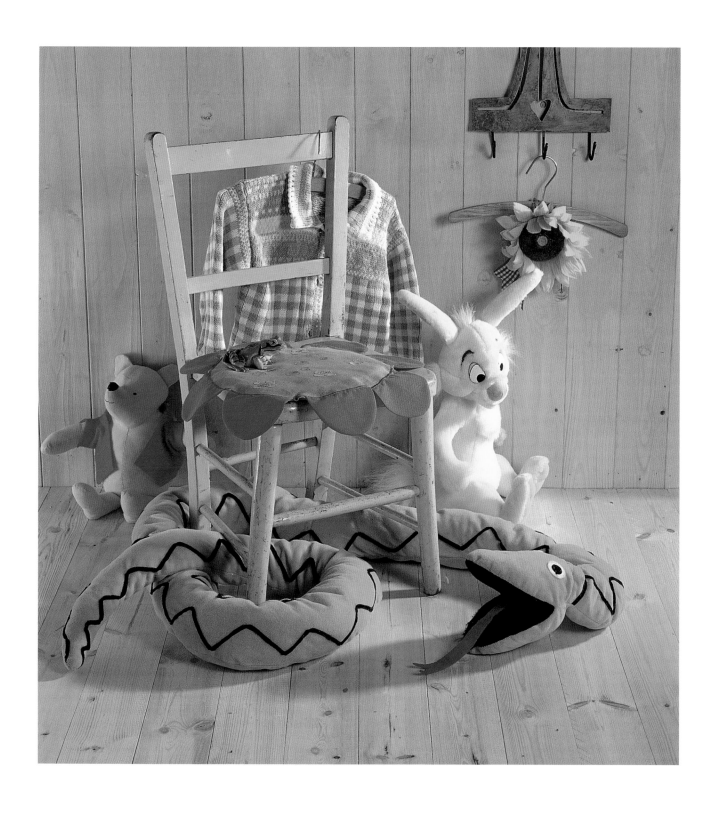

# *Appliqué peapod*

The checked and gingham fabrics used to make up the front of this cushion combine to give a strong country feel. When selecting your fabrics (including the appliqué scraps), make sure they are compatible for washing together and that the colours do not run. The fringed canvas adds to the country feel but if you prefer a neater edge, turn the edges of this fabric under. An embroidered ladder stitch (see page 19) could be sewn around the canvas panel for an alternative look (see the stencilled pig on page 00, for example).

Sew together four squares of patterned fabric to make up the top of the cushion cover. Make this to the required size of the cushion, plus 2.5cm/1in all around for the seam allowance. Sew the pieces together and press the seams open at the back. Cut a plain piece of canvas or cotton to make up the back of the cushion taking into account your preferred method of closing (see pages 80-1). Finally, cut a piece of canvas to fit over the centre of the cushion and fringe around the edges by teasing the threads away with your fingers.

To make the appliqué vegetables, assemble scraps of fabric and cut them roughly to size, using the peapod or carrot outlines on page 93 as a guide (if necessary, enlarge them on a photocopier to an appropriate size). Remember to include a seam allowance around each piece for turning under (see page 21). Juggle the scraps of fabric around until you are satisfied with the arrangement and then pin them in place. Sew the appliqué pieces onto the canvas using tiny ladder stitches (see page 19). Then twist a 10cm/4in piece of cord to resemble the peapod stalk (see the photograph opposite) and pin this onto the canvas. Secure the cord using tiny overstitches.

When the appliqué is complete, pin and then sew the canvas square onto the front of the cushion cover, keeping the stitching line close to the fringed edge.

Sew the front and back parts of the cushion together, with right sides facing and raw edges even. Turn to the right side, press the seams and fill with an appropriate cushion pad (see page 15).

*Left* Assemble small pieces of fabric and pin these onto the canvas. Use orange scraps for a carrot and green scraps for a peapod.

*Right* Coordinating country fabrics make up the main part of the cushion, and the appliqué panel is sewn over these.

# Decorated linen squares

Nine squares stitched together make a generous-sized floor cushion, but if you would prefer to make a smaller cushion, reduce the number of squares. Cut them from two different fabrics to achieve the strong chequerboard effect shown here. The crown motif will be more prominent if it is stitched over a plain fabric.

Decide on the size of your cushion and divide the length of one side by three to determine the size of each patchwork square. Add 1.2cm/½in seam allowances on each side and cut out a paper template using these measurements. Use the template to cut out the fabric squares. Sew the squares together using the sewing machine and maintaining even 1.2cm/½in seam allowances. Press the seams open on the reverse with a warm iron as you progress.

To make the gold crowns, fuse a strip of fusible webbing onto the reverse of a piece of gold fabric. Enlarge the crown template on page 91 on a photocopier to an appropriate size or then transfer it onto paper (see page 11). Pin the template onto the right side of the gold fabric, draw around the shape and cut out. Repeat until enough crowns are cut to correspond with the number of plain squares.

Lightly mark the centre of each square with tailor's chalk. Remove the backing paper from the reverse of each crown to reveal the sticky underside. Then position each one centrally over the plain squares using the chalk marks as a guide and iron in place. Use gold thread and tiny overstitches to sew gold braid around the edge of each crown.

Cut the fabric pieces for the back of the cushion taking into account your preferred method of closing (see pages 12-13). Sew the front and back parts of the cushion together, with right sides facing and raw edges even. Turn to the right side, press the seams and insert an appropriate cushion pad (see page 15).

*Left* Sew gold cord around the edges of the crowns using a metallic thread.

*Right* Sew plain fabric squares alongside patterned ones to create the chequerboard effect.

# Fun with fabric

*Sew wonderful fringes and braids onto your existing cushion covers or use them to add character to new ones. Pile lots of cushions together to make a welcoming stack to fall into, or display a single cover on a favourite chair - whatever you choose, these designs will bring charm to any room.*

# Deckle-edged cushion

The eyecatching edging on this cushion is simply made from remnants of fabric. Once the zigzags are stitched and turned right side out, they are then sewn inside the front and back parts of the cushion. When the cushion is turned right sides out the deckle edging is revealed.

Cut the fabric pieces for the front and back of the cushion taking into account your preferred method of closing (see pages 12-13). The damask fabric that was used here tends to fray so either use pinking shears to cut the fabric or stitch around all the raw edges using a zigzag stitch on the sewing machine.

For the deckle edging, cut four strips of fabric 10cm/4in wide and long enough to stretch along each side of the cushion. Fold each one in half across the length, right sides facing, and press. Enlarge the edging template on page 91 on a photocopier to an appropriate size (my cushion is 40cm/16in square and each point is 5cm/2in wide at its base) or transfer it onto paper (see page 11). Pin the template over the strips of fabric, pointed ends towards the folds, and draw around the outlines using a piece of tailor's chalk. As each set of zigzags is drawn onto the fabric, unpin the template and move it along the strip. Match the chalk lines each time and then repin the template.

Sew the zigzags, using the chalk lines as a stitching guide. At each point of the zigzag, make sure the needle of the sewing machine is down through the thickness of fabric and then raise the foot. Turn the fabric by hand and then lower the foot to progress the line of stitching. Cut away the excess fabric and snip into the corners using a sharp pair of scissors. Finally, turn each zigzag to the right side and press the line of trimming.

Sandwich the deckle-edged trimmings between the front and back of the cushion with right sides facing and raw edges aligned. Pin, then tack along each side and machine stitch in place. Turn right sides out and tug each zigzag gently to shape, then press and fill with an appropriate cushion pad (see page 15).

*Right* Red damask with orange linen deckle edging makes an eyecatching combination.

# Woven ribbons

Choose an assortment of colourful ribbons to coordinate with your existing furnishings or select ribbons that simply catch your eye. To make sure the colours work well together, and before you buy the ribbons, it is a good idea to pull a short length from each one and lay them next to each other. It can be very effective mixing textures as well as patterns and colours, so select velvet and satin ribbons. Different widths of ribbon will also look good.

The ribbon weave is featured on the front of the cushion only, so make this first. Cut a rectangle from a piece of medium/heavyweight iron-on interfacing to the size of your cushion, plus 2.5cm/1in all around for turning. This material can be purchased from fabric departments or haberdashery stores and is usually sold by the metre; avoid lightweight interfacing as this will be too flimsy.

Lay the interfacing on a flat surface with the textured (sticky) side uppermost. Cut your ribbons to the size of the interfacing, remembering that if you are making a rectangular cushion you will need to cut two different lengths of ribbon. Pin the horizontal ribbons in place using pins at either end to secure. Butt the ribbons up closely against each other as this will help the final appearance of the weaving. Once all the horizontal ribbons are in place start to weave the vertical ones.

To start this, pin the first ribbon at the top left or right corner and weave it between the horizontal ones. Pin at the opposite end. Continue until all the spaces are filled with ribbon and you are satisfied with the overall look. Turn the woven fabric over onto an ironing board and press to fuse the ribbons, remove the pins.

Choose and cut a rich velvet, brocade or damask backing fabric taking into account your preferred method of closing (see pages 12-13). Sew the front and back parts of the cushion together, with right sides facing and raw edges even. Turn right side out and fill with an appropriate cushion pad (see page 15).

*Left* Back the ribbon cushion with a rich, heavy cotton velvet.

*Right* Remnants of all kinds of ribbon can be used to make this beautiful cushion.

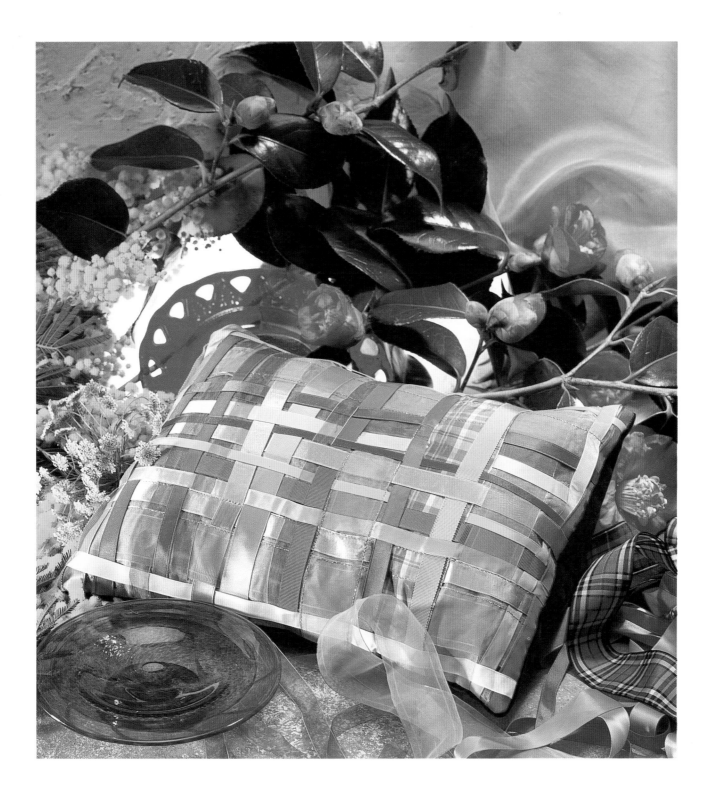

# Damask piped squab

Cushions that are made to fit a chair perfectly make a seat truly comfortable. This seat cushion is filled with foam (see page 15) rather than conventional hollow fibre or feathers for a cushion that will hold its shape and provide most comfort.

Cut a paper pattern for the seat cushion (see page 14). Pin the template onto a double thickness of fabric (right sides facing) and cut out the top and bottom pieces for the cushion. Prepare the piping cord from strips of bias (see page 17). You will need enough piping to go around both the top and bottom of the cushion plus an extra 5cm/2in on each length for joining.

For the welt and using the size measurements from the template (not the chair), cut out four side sections each 7½cm/3in wide plus 1.5cm/⅝in each end for seams. Pin the piping to the top and bottom pieces keeping raw edges together and right sides facing. Keep the piping joins to the back of the cushion and snip the piping to turn each corner. Sew in place using the zipper foot of the sewing machine.

Sew four long ties. As a guide for the length of each one, twist a cloth tape around one of the chair's legs. Cut 5cm/2in-wide strips from the fabric for each tie, and sew across the long side and one short side trapping a piece of string inside the tie. Pull the end of the string to turn the tie to the right side, cut off the string and sew the ends closed. Press each tie and fold in half. Then pin each fold against the raw edges on the base of the cushion fabric at each corner and with the loose ends facing the centre of the cushion. Secure with a couple of stitches and remove the pins.

Pin the edges of the welt to the edges of the cushion, top and bottom, keeping the right sides to the inside. Align the seams at the four corners. Sew, following the stitching line made when inserting the piping cord. Leave a gap for turning, this should also be large enough to place the foam inside. Trim all the seams. Turn right sides out, insert one or two layers of foam (depending on their thickness, see page 15) and stitch the opening closed.

*Left* Leave a small gap open at the back of the cover large enough to slide the piece of foam inside.

*Right* Ties not only look good but they keep the cushion in place as well: make them extra long so that they wind down the chairlegs a little.

# *Ohio star patchwork*

This style of patchwork is made up of small pieces of interlocking fabric that fit together like a jigsaw. The star design is a traditional one but you could make up your own patterns on graph paper and then cut out the pieces. Look at quilts in museums, shops, even magazines or books for your inspiration.

Depending on whether you want one star on the face of your cushion or the four as featured here, enlarge the star motif template on page 94 on a photocopier to an appropriate size. Then transfer the motif onto graph paper (see page 11). Use a sharp pencil and a ruler to draw the star on the graph paper and then cut out each shape separately. You may wish to mark each shape to indicate which pieces join together (see page 22). Select your fabrics carefully. They should all be a similar weight and the colours should be fast; if in doubt wash the fabrics before sewing. Also avoid any fabrics that may shrink.

Pin the paper templates onto the wrong side of the fabric and cut out each piece adding a narrow margin around the edges for turning. Fold the allowance over the paper and tack these in place. Make up all the fabric pieces in this way (see page 22).

To make up the patchwork, place two adjoining pieces together, right sides facing, and use tiny stitches to sew together (the stitch should be barely visible on the right side). Continue stitching in this way, slowly building up the star pattern. Remove the tacking threads, press, remove the paper templates and then tack along the sides of the square to hold the allowances in place.

Sew three more stars in this way and then stitch them all together. Choose and cut a backing fabric taking into account your preferred method of closing (see pages 12-13). Sew the front and back parts of the cushion together, with right sides facing and raw edges even. Turn right side out and fill with an appropriate cushion pad (see page 15).

*Right* Blue and yellow printed cotton
fabrics in different combinations make up
this traditional patchwork design.

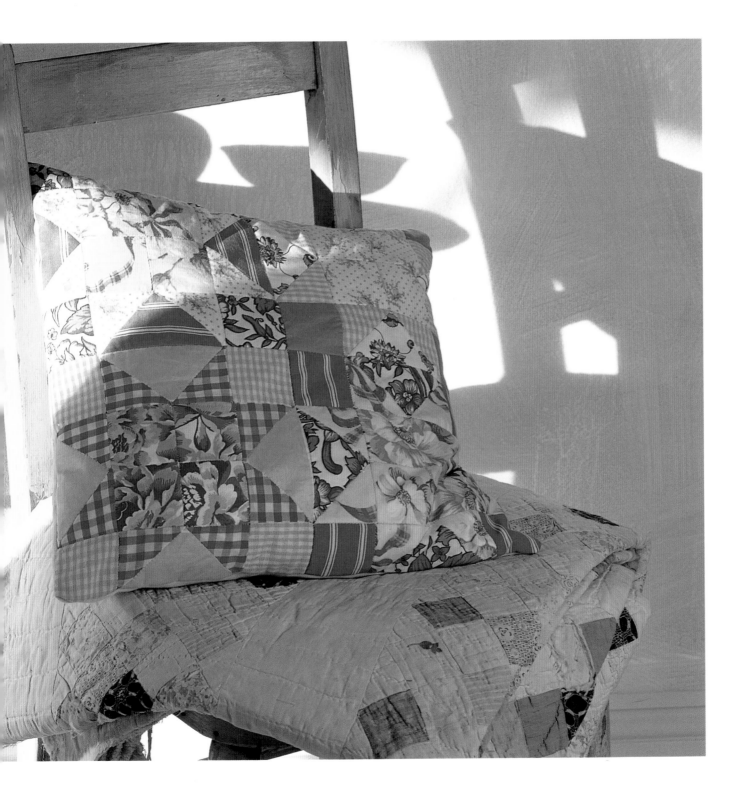

# Scented gingham cushion

This is a frilled cushion made from a lightweight cotton gingham - avoid heavier fabrics as the frills are best very full and soft. The lace panel that decorates the front of the cushion is, in fact, a tray cloth that is stitched onto the front of the cover. You could use an antique handkerchief, a small piece of lace, or a decorative napkin if you wished. It may be a good solution for displaying a favourite piece of lace that would otherwise be hidden in a drawer.

Cut the fabric pieces for the front and back of the cushion taking into account the method of closing (see pages 12-13). Your piece of chosen lace will determine the size of the cushion: as a guide, measure the panel and add 5cm/2in all around for a border and allowances. Also cut long strips of the gingham fabric 15cm/7½in wide for the frilled edge. In order to achieve the soft gathered look, you will need to cut and join together enough strips to go around the outside edge of the cushion twice. You may need to join several lengths to get the long piece you require in which case stitch together the pieces with a flat seam and press it open at the back.

Fold the strip in half across the width and press and then sew the strip end to end, making one continuous loop. Sew double running stitches close to the raw edges of the strip (see page 18) and pin the strip onto the four corners on the face fabric, keeping the raw edges even. There will be twice the length of strip between each pin. Start to pull the gathering threads slowly, teasing the folds gently between your fingers, evening out the frills. Pin and then stitch.

Pin and then stitch the lace panel onto the cushion front fabric. Sew the front and back parts of the cushion together, with right sides facing and raw edges even. Turn right side out and fill with a potpourri bag and appropriate cushion pad (see page 15).

*Left* The scent of lavender diffuses through a muslin bag that is placed inside the cushion together with the pad. Use ready-prepared potpourri or, for a really wonderful fragrance, rub the dried flower heads from a bunch of freshly dried lavender.

*Right* A simple lace panel is stitched over the front of this frilled cushion.

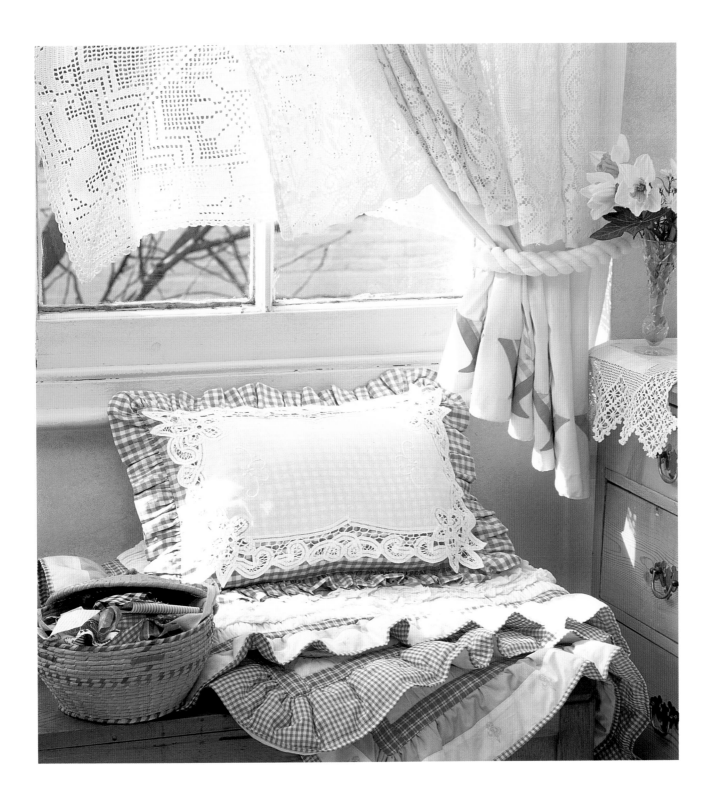

# Bean bag frog

This giant oversized frog floor cushion is inspired by a smaller variety that is much loved by my small daughter. I have used two different types of stuffing inside the frog; the feet are filled with a soft hollow fibre and the legs and body are filled with polystyrene balls to make the frog more animated.

Enlarge the frog template on page 92 on a photocopier to an appropriate size .or transfer it onto paper (see page 11) and follow the instructions on pages 12-13 for making shaped cushions. Cut out the paper template and pin it onto a double thickness of fabric folded with right sides facing. I used a bright green linen for this frog cushion, but don't feel that because the cushion has a frog character it should necessarily be green.

Remove the template and pin the two pieces of fabric together. Pin at right angles to the raw edges to allow the sewing foot on the sewing machine to stitch over them. Stitch around the frog leaving a small seam allowance. Due to the inevitable rough handling the cushion will be subjected to (I know ours is), I advise sewing a double row of stitches around the seams for added strength. Leave a small gap for filling.

Snip the curves with a sharp pair of scissors, cutting almost up to the line of stitching. Turn the frog right sides out and stuff, first with the hollow fibre in the feet and then with the polystyrene balls - but don't pack the polystyrene into the frog tightly as the frog needs to bend and move around. There's no real easy way to fill the frog with the balls, just pour them into the upturned frog. Sew the hole closed using strong thread and stitch beads on for eyes.

*Left* Fill the feet with soft hollow fibre to hold their shape and the body with polystyrene balls.

*Above* This bean bag frog makes a really unusual floor cushion. If this frog is being made for a baby or small child, it is advisable to oversew two embroidery thread eyes on top of the frog's head, rather than using beads which may be pulled off.

# Harlequin bolster

The two-tone decoration for this cushion uses a basic patchwork method. The squares are stitched together to form a flat piece of fabric which is then rolled into a cylinder to fit around a feather bolster pad.

First choose your two fabrics. They should be compatible for washing together, and pre-shrunk and colourfast. Then cut a 10cm/4in template from stiff card. Lay it onto the wrong side of one of the fabrics and use a light pencil to draw around the sides. Repeat for as many times as you need squares and then cut them out. Repeat on the contrasting-colour fabric. I cut out about 30 for my 50cm/20in-long bolster.

Stitch the squares together maintaining an even seam allowance of 6mm/¼in to prevent distortion. It is a good idea to first stitch together a number of squares in pairs, then four squares, then eight and so on - always alternating the colours, of course - ending up with, say, three pieces that are then sewn together into one large piece of harlequin fabric.

The length of the patchwork will eventually need to match the length of the bolster, plus 2.5cm/1in for seams, and the width should equal the circumference of the pad plus 2.5cm/1in seam allowance. However, as the patchwork is displayed on the diagonal to give the characteristic harlequin pattern you will need to make a piece of patchwork that is larger than these measurements and then trim it on the diagonal to the right size.

*Above* Tie the ends of the bolster rather like a huge Christmas cracker.

*Left* To make the triangular ties, fold four corners of a 5cm/2in-square piece of fabric to the centre and press. Place the ties over the raw edges, fold, and then sew.

Sew a rectangle of plain fabric 25cm/10in wide to either end of the patchwork, trim to the patchwork width and turn under the raw edges at the ends using a double hem.

To join the patchwork tube, and to ensure correct alignment of the diamonds, pin the fabric together wrapped around the pad and with the wrong side uppermost. Slide the pad out and then stitch the seam.

Make two ties for the bolster from strips of fabric 5cm/2in wide. Using the string method for turning (see page 48), fold each strip in half widthways and sew along two sides. Enclose the raw ends with a triangle of folded fabric (see caption opposite, bottom) and finally bind each strip around each end of the bolster to pull the excess fabric together. Tie in a firm knot to prevent them from coming undone.

# Spotted stegosaurus

This eyecatching stegosaurus uses a similar piece of zigzag edging as used for the deckle-edged cushion at the beginning of this chapter (see pages 44-5), but here it is set along the top edge of the cushion to resemble the platelets on a stegosaurus's back.

Enlarge the stegosaurus template on page 91 on a photocopier to an appropriate size (my cushion is 76cm/30in long) or transfer it onto paper (see page 11). Cut out the template and pin it onto a double thickness of fabric folded with the right sides facing. Cut out the fabric, remove the template and pin the two pieces together but leave the back unpinned for the zigzag edging. Pin at right angles to the raw edges to allow the sewing foot on the sewing machine to stitch over them.

Stitch together a strip of contrasting fabric for the platelets on the stegosaurus's back, following the method outlined for the deckle-edge cushion on page 44, but this time enlarge the template on page 91 so that each point is 7.5cm/3in wide at the base. Turn the points along the trimming to the right side and press carefully. Trim the raw edges so they are even and set this edging along the back of the shaped stegosaurus, between the front and back pieces of fabric. Keep the raw edges even and the points to the inside. Pin as before and then stitch, leaving a small, even seam allowance all around the edges. Leave a small gap at the bottom for turning. Turn the stegosaurus, right sides out, tugging the points gently to even these out.

For the colourful spots on the stegosaurus's back, iron a piece of fusible webbing to the reverse side of a piece of contrasting coloured fabric. Cut out small dots, remove the protective paper backing from each spot, and then place them onto the cushion. Iron in place; the sticky glue is activated by heat.

Sew on buttons for the eyes, and fill using a synthetic filling (see page 15). For babies, check the filling meets all the relevant safety checks. Sew the gap closed with strong thread.

*Right* Prop the cushion against a pillow in a small child's bedroom or around the sides of a cot.

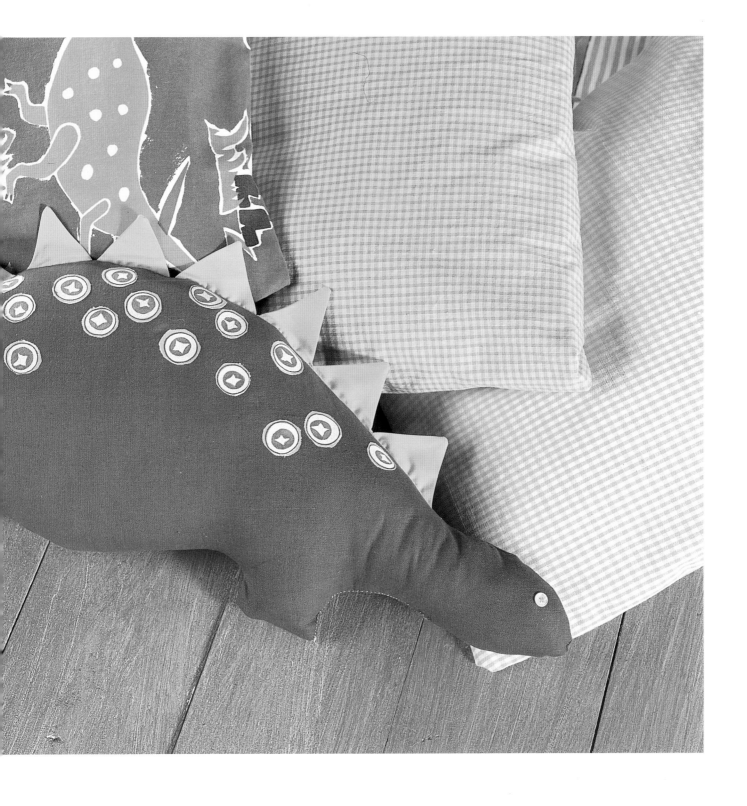

# Velvet roses and leaves

This unusual-shaped cushion has a red velvet diamond stitched over a diamond-shaped tomato red cotton cover. The lines of stitching are covered with exquisite tiny red velvet roses and green leaves for a really delightful cushion that could be propped up against the pillows on a bed or against the back of a sofa.

Cut the fabric pieces for the front and back of the cushion taking into account your preferred method of closing (see pages 12-13). Make it diamond-shaped and use a template for cutting, following the daisy shaped seat pad instructions on page 36. Use a regular cotton duck fabric, as I have here, or for a richer look use damask or chintz. Then cut a diamond from the red velvet using the same paper template made for the cover, less 7.5cm/3in all around.

Pin and then sew the velvet diamond onto the centre of the front face fabric using a close zigzag stitch to seal the raw edges. Sew the front and back pieces of the cushion together, right sides facing, then turn to the right side through the back opening and gently press on the back of the cushion.

For the flowers, use 7.5cm/3in-wide red velvet ribbon, and for the leaves, use 5cm/2in-wide green velvet ribbon. Fold a 20cm/8in strip of red ribbon in half widthways, velvet sides outside, and start to roll up the flower head. Bunch the ribbon occasionally to form natural-looking flowers. Fold the raw edge underneath and use long stabbing stitches to secure the rose head. Repeat, making enough roses to cover the stitching lines around the cushion.

To make the leaves, fold a 15cm/6in piece of the velvet ribbon in half lengthways, right sides out, and pin. Select a close zigzag stitch on the sewing machine and thread with green cotton. Sew a diamond shape across the double ribbon and cut away the excess velvet. Sew across the centre of these leaves to gather the velvet and create the leaf shape.

Using invisible stitches, attach the leaves and roses around the line of machine stitching. Using the paper template, make a diamond-shaped muslin pad (see page 15) and fill it with the appropriate filling (also see page 15). Remove the pad prior to cleaning.

*Left* Make lots of roses and leaves from velvet ribbons first and then sew them around the edge of the cushion.

*Right* Luxurious red velvet is used on the front of the cushion and decorated with velvet flowers.

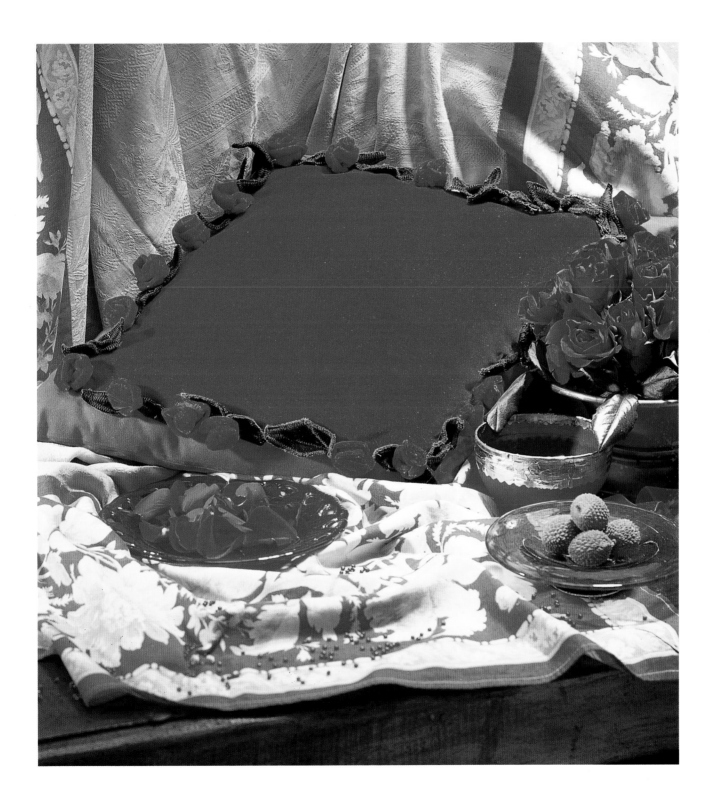

# Tartan rosettes cushion

Tartan fabrics are enjoying a revival at the moment and quite rightly so. These beautiful and intricate plaids can be seen on carpets, cabinets, cushions and upholstery. The small rectangular cushion here is designed to support the neck but the number of squares used can be changed to suit your requirements. Stitch nine squares to make a large floor cushion or four squares for a regular-shaped scatter cushion.

Cut as many tartan squares (or halves) as are required for the front of the cushion, adding 2.5cm/1in all around each one for seam allowances. Attach the decorative detailing before stitching the fabric together. I have used a cross of tartan ribbon across each square, or part thereof. Choose contrasting tartan ribbons, but ensure that the width of each ribbon is the same so the crosses match evenly where they meet. This is particularly important if your cushion has four or more tartan squares. Pin the lengths of ribbon in place with a single pin across each ribbon end.

Pin the squares of fabric together with right sides facing and raw edges even. Check to see if the ribbons align, adjusting if necessary by re-pinning. Sew the squares together and press the seams open. Choose the back fabric and cut out taking into account your preferred method of closing (see pages 12-13). Sew the front and back parts of the cushion together, with right sides facing and raw edges even. Turn right sides out, remove the pins and press.

To make the rosettes, take 50cm/20in of 4cm/1½in-wide ribbon and make a series of tiny concertina pleats along the length. Press each fold with a warm iron to hold. As four or five pleats are made, secure their base with a running stitch (see page 18). When the pleating is finished, gently pull the running stitch thread to gather the base of the folds and form the rosettes. Stitch the ends of the ribbon together and hand stitch a rosette to the centre of each tartan square where the tartan ribbons cross. For each half rosette, halve the length of ribbon and form this into a semi-circle. Finish the cushion off with self-covered buttons (see page 86) positioned in the centre of each rosette and fill with an appropriate cushion pad (see page 15).

*Left* When making each tartan rosette, pull the ends of the thread to draw up the pleats.

*Right* The rectangular cushion is designed to fit neatly into the nape of the neck to support the head.

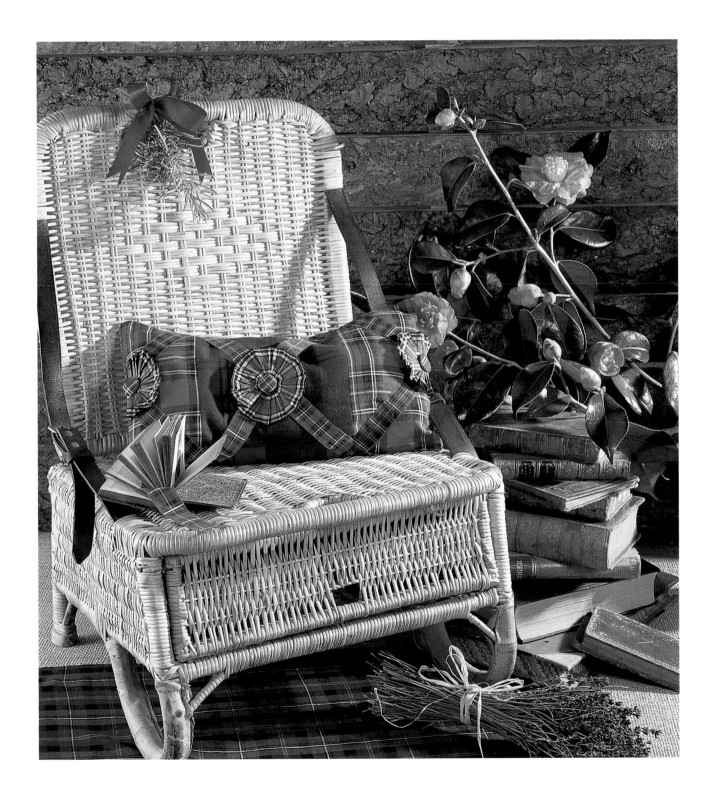

# Piped cushions

A simple row of piping adds definition to a cushion and can make a world of difference. Throughout the pages of this book you will notice several different edgings, be it a double piped edge as on the star-stamped cushion (see page 76) or gathered piping as seen on the stencilled pig cushion (see page 81). The three cushions you see here each have a different kind of piping detail, too - a multi-coloured twisted cord, simple piping, and a combination of cord and piping.

Piping cord comes in a number of thicknesses. Generally, I use one of the thicker cords for edging, unless the cushions are unusually small, when I would use a finer cord. The sizing of cords varies from number 00 which is very fine through to number 6 which, not surprisingly, is the thickest.

By using piping cord alone you can quickly and easily embellish an existing cushion. Simply hand sew a cord around the seam of the cushion, adding a loop at the corners for further detailing if required. To join the ends of the piping cord together unravel each end slightly and then twist them back together. Firmly stitch the join to avoid unravelling; I use several overstitches to catch the silky threads firmly in place which will spoil the cord if it unravels.

For a row of single piping see page 17 for making instructions. To bring a touch of originality to rows of single piping, you might try alternating different colours or textures of fabric. Alternatively, reverse the fabrics used on the cushions featured opposite - use brightly patterned pipings on plain cushion covers. These sorts of pipings would be perfect accompaniments for plain coloured fabric cushions as they would enliven them in a most refreshing way.

An alternative edging uses both a cord and a row of single piping, as shown below. Make up a cushion inserting a contrasting piped edge, as before. Then add the cord, making a loop at each corner and stitching it in place for an attractive finish.

*Left* Hand stitch decorative cord close to the piped edge for an unusual double piping.

*Right* Edge cushions with hand-made piping or purchased cord.

# Tasselled tapestry cushion

A quick look at the price tag on any authentic tapestry cushion will leave you speechless: they do command the highest prices. However, a stroll down the racks of most upholstery fabrics will reveal some very beautiful tapestry-effect fabrics, which are positive bargains. Most of these fabrics are soft, muted colours, so a naturally coloured trimming would be perfectly suited to the cushion edging. Determine the size of your cushion and purchase the relevant amount of fabric, allowing 2.5cm/1in all around for seams. To make several tapestry cushions, select a plain canvas backing fabric so that several cushions can be made from only a small amount of tapestry fabric.

To make the cushion, cut the cotton fabric to the size of the cushion, adding 2.5cm/1in all around for seam allowances. Measure the width of your trimming plus 2cm/3/4in and 2.5cm/1in allowance for the seams to determine the width of plain border to be left around the tapestry fabric in the centre of the cushion. Measure,

then cut a piece of the tapestry to fit the space. Pin the tapestry fabric centrally onto the right side of the cotton fabric. Then hand stitch it in place, keeping the raw edges turned under as you progress. You may find it easier to press this small seam under using an iron prior to stitching to ensure the allowances are even.

With right sides facing and using a complementary coloured thread, sew on the trimming with tiny hand stitches (see page 16). At the corners, fold the trimming neatly to form mitred edges (see below). Do not be tempted to cut the trimming as this may lead to fraying once the cushion is cleaned at a later date.

Choose the base fabric and cut out taking into account your preferred method of closing (see pages 12-13). Sew the front and back parts of the cushion together, with right sides facing and raw edges even. Turn right sides out and press out the corners using the blunt end of a knitting needle. Fill with an appropriate cushion pad (see page 15).

*Left*  For a neat finish fold the trimming into small mitred corners.

*Right*  A rectangle of tapestry-effect fabric has been stitched on top of a cotton fabric, the colour of which complements the tapestry. A natural-coloured trimming is stitched around the edge. Unusually, the trimming lies flat around the face of the cushion rather than decorating the edge in a more traditional way.

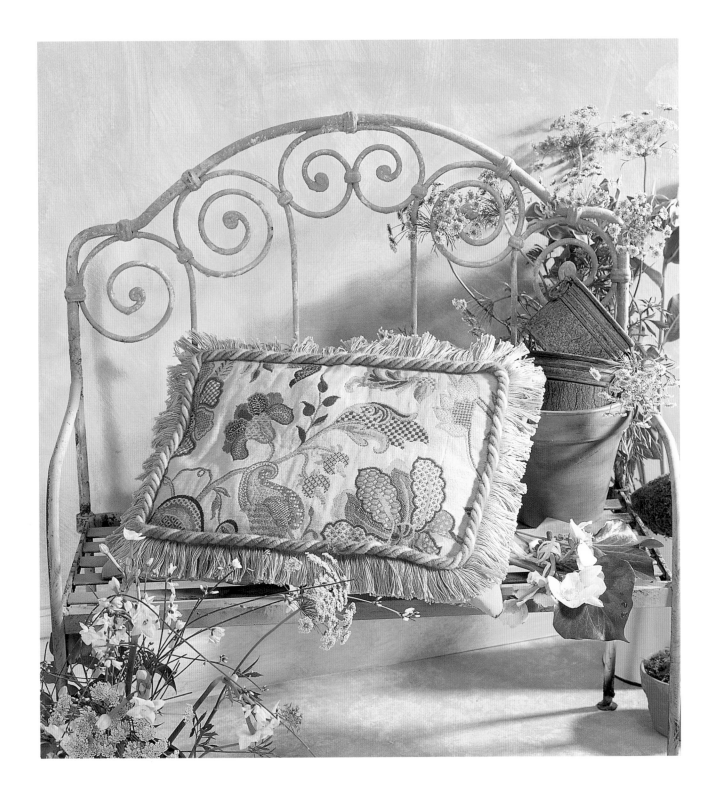

# Buttoned squabs

Buttons can easily be covered in the same fabric as a cushion pad and used to provide a decorative detailing on the front of the cushion. If you are making more than one cushion, as I have done here, select different fabric for each one but link them by colour. I used three different blue and white fabrics, and finished off each one with a different arrangement of buttons - one button in the centre on one cushion, and five and nine buttons grouped across the fronts of the other two.

Cut a top and bottom for the cushion cover using the chair seat as a guide (see page 14), remembering to include a 2.5cm/1in seam allowance all around. The cushion is stitched closed so the front and back pieces are exactly the same. If the seat base is shaped, cut a template for the fabric pieces using newspaper or brown paper. Place the paper over the seat and cut around the sides. Fold the template in half to check the symmetry and trim the paper accordingly. Remember to add the 2.5cm/1in seam allowance when cutting the front and back pieces from the fabric.

Piping gives a neat edge to these cushions. Cut a long bias strip from the same fabric to make a length of piping cord for each cushion and then cover the piping cord (see page 17). Insert the piping into the seam of the cover between the front and back pieces, aligning all raw edges. Snip the seam allowance to turn the piping around each corner. Stitch the layers firmly together leaving a gap along one side for turning. Turn right side out.

For these cushions, I used a foam filling to keep the cushion flat on the chair seat and to provide the most comfort. To insert this type of filling, simply slide the cut foam into the partly opened seam and then stitch the gap closed with neat, small overstitches using a matching coloured thread. The foam is easily cut to size using a sharp craft knife.

Cover the buttons (see page 86) and use a strong thread to sew them onto the cover, stitching through the foam as well as both layers of fabric to create the deeply buttoned look.

*Left* Sew the covered piping between the top and bottom pieces of the cushion cover.

*Right* Buttoned squabs soften a hard seat, making it more comfortable to sit on.

# Freestyle cushions

*Among the many designs here, you will find a mixture of various techniques to appeal to most tastes and for every room. Sew a simple cushion cover in one evening or take your time over one of the more elaborate ones.*

# *Ribbon-edged cushion*

For a unique edging detail, four lengths of wide satin ribbon are threaded through four channels of fabric stitched around the edges of this cushion and tied in a bow. A panelled fabric, as used here, is effective for this cushion, but the cushion could be made from almost any other fabric to suit your requirements. A white lace cushion threaded with broad white ribbon would look pretty in a bedroom, or a needlepoint cushion threaded with velvet ribbon would look stunning in a living room.

Cut the fabric pieces for the front and back of the cushion taking into account your preferred method of closing (see pages 12-13). To make the channels to hold the lengths of ribbon, cut 7.5cm/3in strips of a contrasting fabric to correspond with the sides of the cushion. Fold over 2.5cm/1in at each end of the four strips and press. Fold each strip in half widthways and with right sides out to make a long, thin strip.

With the face fabric in front of you, pin the four channels along the four corresponding edges of the cushion, keeping raw edges even and right sides together. Pin at right angles to the raw edges to allow the sewing foot on the sewing machine to stitch over them. Sew the channels in place maintaining an even seam allowance of 2.5cm/1in. Pin then sew the base fabric over this, keeping to the same line of stitches. Trim the seams, turn the cushion to the right side and carefully press with a warm iron.

Cut each piece of ribbon to the same length as the channels plus 50cm/20in to form plump bows at each corner. Thread one end of the ribbon into a thick, round-ended needle (or compromise with a safety pin) and pass a ribbon through each channel allowing 25cm/10in to hang down at either side. Once all four ribbons are threaded, tie each corner into a neat bow. Fill with an appropriate cushion pad (see page 15).

*Above* Pin the channels onto the front of the front, keeping raw edges even.

*Right* Tie the ribbons into generous bows at each corner.

# Buttoned lacy cushions

Lots of pearly buttons are used to decorate the borders of these cushions. I was lucky enough to find a whole jar of buttons in a junk shop - probably a lifetime's collection of odd assortments cut from old shirts and blouses: what a treasure. So rather than keeping these hidden away I decided to show them off and the buttons look wonderful sewn next to each other around these pretty bedroom cushions. If your collection of buttons is a little more modest, sew a single row around the lace panel or simply make smaller cushions.

Cut the fabric pieces for the front and back of the cushion taking into account your preferred method of closing (see pages 12-13). If you decide to make a shaped cushion see the instructions on pages 14-15. Set aside the back parts as all the decoration is worked on the front.

Cut a lace panel for the front of each cushion using the same measurements as for the cushion front less 10cm/4in all around. Pin this panel onto the centre of the cushion front, pinning at right angles to the raw edges to allow the stitching foot on the sewing machine to pass over them. Then stitch around the edges using a close zigzag stitch on your sewing machine to tidy all the raw edges. Remove the pins.

Hand stitch the buttons around the lace panel to create a deep or narrow border, depending on the number of buttons you have to hand. To create interest around the border, sew large buttons next to small ones, and pretty ones next to plain ones. Any unique or highly decorated buttons should be given prominence and sewn at the centre of the borders. Cover the zigzag stitching line as you progress.

Sew the front and back parts of the cushion together, with right sides facing and raw edges even. Trim the corners and then turn right sides out. If one of the cushions is circular, notch around the seam allowance prior to turning to the right side to make the seam less bulky. On the back of the cushion press the seams flat using a warm iron and insert an appropriate cushion pad (see page 15).

*Left* Hand sew a lace trimming around the edges of the cushion using small, discreet stitches.

*Right* A collection of buttons are far more interesting when displayed around the edges of these pretty bedroom cushions.

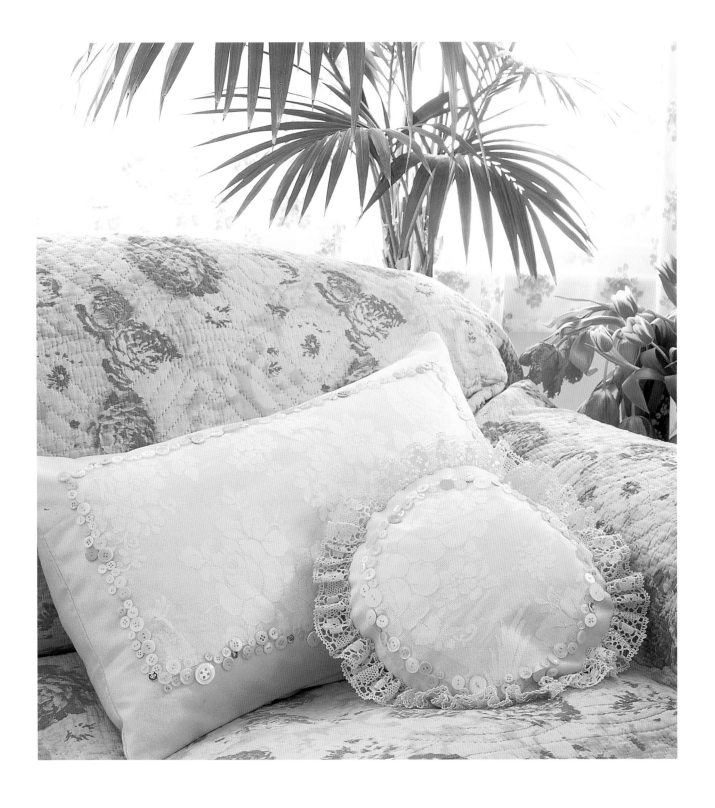

# Star-stamped cushion

Fabric stamps are great fun to use and the character of each print varies slightly, due to the pressure applied when printing. As a result, this characteristic sets the decoration apart from manufactured prints that are unfailingly regular, adding an altogether most attractive, hand-printed quality.

Cut a piece of fabric for the face of your cushion; I used a pale yellow raw silk fabric to highlight the gold fabric paint. Then divide the fabric into 7.5cm/3in squares, marking each square lightly with white chalk (tailor's chalk is ideal as this has a narrow marking edge). Also mark the centre of each square to provide a positioning guide for the star stamp.

Roll out a little of the fabric paint onto a flat surface; an old glazed tile, plate or piece of glass would do. Cover a small roller with the paint and then transfer the paint onto the printing block. Press the block over the marked spot. Hold for a few seconds and remove the stamp to reveal each star. Don't worry if the star has lost any detailing - I think it adds to the hand-printed effect - and never put the stamp back onto the fabric as it is difficult to re-align the design.

Continue until the fabric is printed and then leave it to dry. You may need to fix the paint with an iron, check the paint information.

Cut the base fabric taking into account your preferred method of closing (see pages 12-13). For a professional finish, insert a double piped edge setting a narrow covered piping in front of a wider one and keeping the raw edges even (see page 17 for making piping). Pin, tack and then sew both cords together onto the back of the cushion, snipping the piping at the corners to turn. Sew the cushion pieces together and turn the right side out. Carefully press using a piece of cotton fabric between the iron and cushion cover and then fill with an appropriate cushion pad (see page 15).

*Left* Use special fabric paints for printing onto cushion covers.

*Right* A double piping edge gives a neat, crisp edge to this cushion.

# *Fringed and trimmed cushions*

There are lots and lots of different trimmings that can be purchased to decorate new or existing cushions. The only limitation you may have is price as some exquisite, handmade passementerie will require a bank loan, whereas others are decidedly more affordable. Look out for small lengths of trimmings in remnant bags at large stores. These are often greatly reduced and frequently contain a length perfectly suited for trimming a single cushion. Antique shops and occasionally thrift shops can unearth similar hidden treasures. I can never resist a rummage through the dusty old cardboard boxes hidden beneath piles of junk as occasionally I am rewarded with a selection of tattered trimmings bundled together with a thick elastic band.

Some trimmings need to be stitched between the front and back cushion pieces (see page 16) and are therefore really only practical when used for sewing a new cushion, unless you want to unpick the stitching from an old cushion cover to inset the trimming. Yet, even so, beware. On some old cushions, especially old tapestry cushions, it may only be the stitching lines that are holding them together. The ideal solution for an old cushion is to look for a trimming or braid that can be hand stitched around the edge of the cushion.

Often more than one trimming can be used on a cushion to add texture and interest. A twisted cord stitched around the edge of a fringed border, for example, can highlight a tapestry panel or add importance to an otherwise simple fabric. Heavy tassels also look extremely, effective when sewn at the four corners of a cushion.

Two of the cushions shown here feature fringed trimmings that are stitched in place once the cushion is sewn together (see page 16). It is often easier to do this once the pad is inside the cushion. The third, corded, trimming is inserted between the top and bottom parts of the cushion before sewing them together. This type of cord has a woven strip fixed to the cord itself and it is this that is pinned and then stitched between the cushion pieces (also see page 16).

*Above* Hand sew the fringing around the edges of the cushion.

*Right* Use purchased trimmings to add instant flourish to a new or old cushion.

# Stencilled pig cushion

Who could resist these charming cushions? The applique style of stitching used to sew the calico pig panel onto the cushion is perfectly suited to the country fabric used to make the cushion cover.

Enlarge the pig template on page 90 on a photocopier to an appropriate size and then transfer it onto a piece of stencil card. Place the stencil on a suitable cutting surface and use a craft knife to cut out the pig (see page 23). Position the stencil over a piece of calico and secure using small pieces of double-sided tape on the reverse. The calico can be trimmed later according to the size of your cushion but at this stage ensure that the pig is positioned centrally on the fabric and that there is sufficient fabric around the stencil to be cut to size later.

When stencilling, vary the amount of paint applied to some areas of the pig (see also page 23). For example, the larger body area can be patchy whereas the tail and feet should be more heavily worked for definition. Leave the paint to dry and then fix it according to the manufacturer's paint instructions.

Cut the fabric pieces for the front and back of the cushion taking into account your preferred method of closing (see pages 12-13). Then cut back the panel sufficiently so that sits comfortably in the centre of the cushion with a 10cm/4in border of background fabric around it. Stitch the panel centrally onto the top of the cushion cover using a close zigzag stitch on the sewing machine. Sew a deep ladder stitch around the panel using three strands of a complementary-coloured embroidery thread (see page 19).

Make up the cover and for interest stitch a gathered piped edge around the cushion. To do this, make a regular piping case (see page 17) but sew it in place using a long stitch and don't hold the zipper foot too close to the cord. Then tease back the fabric casing gently over the piping cord to give it a ruched appearance. Pin the piping around the right edge of the top cover with raw edges aligned. Snip the piping at the corners to fit and stitch the cover front and back together. Finally, turn the right sides out, press and fill with an appropriate cushion pad (see page 15).

*Left* Vary the pressure used on the stencil brush to build up a more interesting area of colour.

*Right* I love the naive feel of this cute pig, and think that these cushions would look perfect in a child's room or nursery. Once the stencil is cut why restrict yourself to only cushion covers? Substitute the fabric paint for hard surface paint and stencil a matching border around the nursery walls.

# Heart-shaped cushion

Shaped cushions are no more complicated than square ones, as long as you make a template first (see pages 14-15). It is advisable to insert a zip fastening when making shaped cushions, and to insert it into the back cover to avoid fitting it around difficult curves (see page's 12-13).

Enlarge the heart-shaped templates on page 90 on a photocopier to an appropriate size or transfer them onto paper (see page 11). For the front of the cushion, cut out one piece of base fabric using the larger-sized heart template. Then cut the template in half vertically down the centre and prepare the back piece and insert the zip as for the daisy-shaped seat pad on page 36.

To add decorative detailing to the front of the cushion cover, use the smaller heart template to cut out a coordinating piece of fabric. Pin the smaller heart over the larger one, maintaining an even allowance all the way around.

For a striking detailed edging, cut small rows of scalloping from several lengths of blue felt, enough to go all around the edge of the inner heart. Use a coin as a guide to make each scallop and cut the felt using a small pair of sharp scissors. Slide the felt edging between the two hearts and pin securely, butting the felt strips against each other to avoid any gaps.

Sew around the inner heart using a close zigzag stitch and a blue toning thread. Then stitch the two main parts of the cover together with right sides facing and leaving the zip open for turning. Turn the cover to the right side and stitch around the edge of the inner heart using blue thread to match the previous line of stitches. This creates a flat border around the edge of the cushion.

Finally, make a muslin cushion pad using the larger template (see Making your own cushion pad on page 15) and insert in the cushion cover.

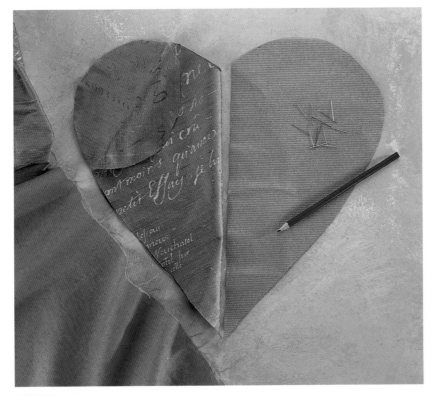

*Left* Use a paper template to cut the fabric to size.

*Right* The bright blue hand-made trimming emphasizes the panel inside the heart cushion.

# *Aran knit cushion*

Almost any pieces of material can be sewn together to make up a cushion cover, including squares cut from an old jumper. Aran jumpers can be bought for very little at junk shops or jumble sales. Wash a woollen jumper in a very hot, soapy wash to felt the wool slightly. Jumpers marked for hand washing only respond to this heavy-handed treatment perfectly as the fibres shrink and the wool takes on a kind of attractive felted appearance. Similar cushions can be made from other woollen items. Scour the junk shops for woollen blankets or shawls, for example. Likewise, a patchwork of woollen squares can be cut from scarves, jumpers or blankets and sewn together for a chequerboard effect.

From a washed and dried jumper, cut the largest squares possible from the body of the garment; generally I find that the sleeves are too narrow to be of any real use. Inserting a zip may be too difficult with woollen fibres and there may not be enough fabric to make an envelope closing, so stitch all sides closed after inserting the cushion pad (see below).

Stitch around three-and-a-half sides taking a regular seam allowance all around. Then select the zigzag facility on your sewing machine and with a longish stitch, zigzag the raw edges together to prevent fraying. Turn right sides out, fill the cushion with an appropriate cushion pad (see page 15) and sew the gap closed.

To add the button detailing, use a wooden toggle at both the front and back of the cushion. Knot a double strand of knitting wool and pass this through the centre of the cushion, pull the needle through, then take a stitch and pass the needle back through to the other side. As the loop gets smaller, catch the toggle in place and pull the yarn tight. Repeat on the first side, trapping another toggle. Wind the wool around each toggle several times before securing with three stitches and cutting off the loose end.

*Left* Cut the largest squares possible from the front and back of the sweater.

*Right* A wooden toggle is sewn onto the front and back of this cushion to complete the look.

# Felt flower fastenings

I love self-covering buttons as you can decorate them in any number of interesting ways. These flower buttons are a real favourite, they crop up on my curtain headings, on upholstery and now on this brightly coloured cushion cover.

Stitch together a regular cushion cover using a simple envelope closing as outlined on pages 7-12. To create the flat border around the outside edge of the cushion simply turn the cover to the right side, pin across its centre to prevent the fabric moving around too much, and sew a stitching line around the inside edge. Leave a regular border of approximately 5cm/2in all around; follow a line on the foot plate of the sewing machine as a guide. To turn the corners check the needle is down through all the layers of fabric, lift the sewing foot, turn the fabric and then depress the sewing foot and continue stitching.

To make the flower buttons, first determine the number of buttons you will need - this will depend on the size of your cushion, but I have made ten. Separate the two halves that make up each button and cut a corresponding number of cotton circles from a pretty fabric. Follow the manufacturer's instructions to cover the top half of the button. Then press the top half together with the bottom half to close.

Cut small flower petals from coloured felt using the template on page 90 transferred onto paper (see page 11). Snip a small slot in the centre of each petal shape and push the wire stitching loop, found at the base of each button, through this. Using a strong sewing thread to attach the buttons onto the cover, sew the buttons along the stitching line made when forming the flat edge detail. Wind the thread around the base of the button several times for added strength before finishing.

Fill the cushion with an appropriate cushion pad (see page 15). If your cushion is an irregular size and you can't find a purchased pad that fits, then make your own (see also page 15).

*Left* Cut tiny petals for the flowers from brightly coloured felt.

*Right* Tiny flowers sewn around the border make an eyecatching trimming on an otherwise plain cushion.

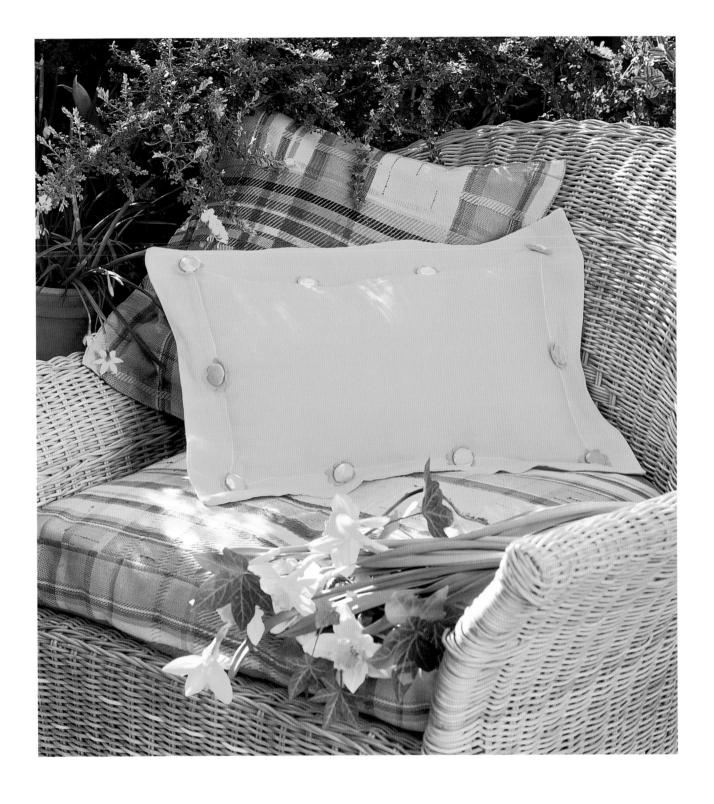

# Organandie pockets

This scented cushion has the real pieces of potpourri trapped beneath a layer of semi-transparent organdie fabric. The inspiration for displaying the scented fruit and flowers came from an exquisite piece of textile design created by Sara Feathers who stitches micro-thin pieces of dried fruit and flowers into her designs. The pieces of pot pourri may be crushed if sat upon but will last indefinitely if propped up among other cushions.

Cut the fabric pieces for the front and back of the cushion taking into account your preferred method of closing (see pages 12-13). Cut a panel of organdie fabric to the same size as the front cover, less 7½cm/3in all around. Use pinking shears if you have them to prevent fraying otherwise turn under a tiny hem and stitch down. Pin the organdie fabric over the top part of the cushion cover and use a ruler and tailor's chalk to divide up the pockets.

Divide each side into three equal sections and then join the marks together horizontally and vertically to create a noughts-and-crosses type chequerboard. Pin the organdie across the centre in several places to prevent the fabric slipping.

Sew along three sides of the organdie and down two vertical lines to create three long pockets that are open at their base. Tip some potpourri ingredients into each of the three pockets making sure it slides down inside the pocket to the end of each channel. Flatten out the fabric and stitch a horizontal line across the cushion enclosing the pot pourri in a neat pocket. Repeat this procedure twice more until nine pockets have been created.

Sew the front and back parts of the cushion together, with right sides facing and raw edges even. Turn the right side out and press.

To add detail to the outside seam, thread a long needle with a strand of raffia and carefully stitch neat loops around the edge of the cushion, knotting each loop before moving to the next. In this way, you will keep the loops even.

*Left* Slide pieces of fruit and vegetable potpourri inside the organdie pockets.

*Right* Complete this unusual cushion with a raffia edging.

# *Templates*

Stencilled pig cushion
(pages 80-1)

Felt flower fastenings
(pages 86-7)

Beaded heart cushion
(pages 28-9)

Appliqué hearts
cushion (pages 34-5)

Heart-shaped cushion
(pages 82-3)

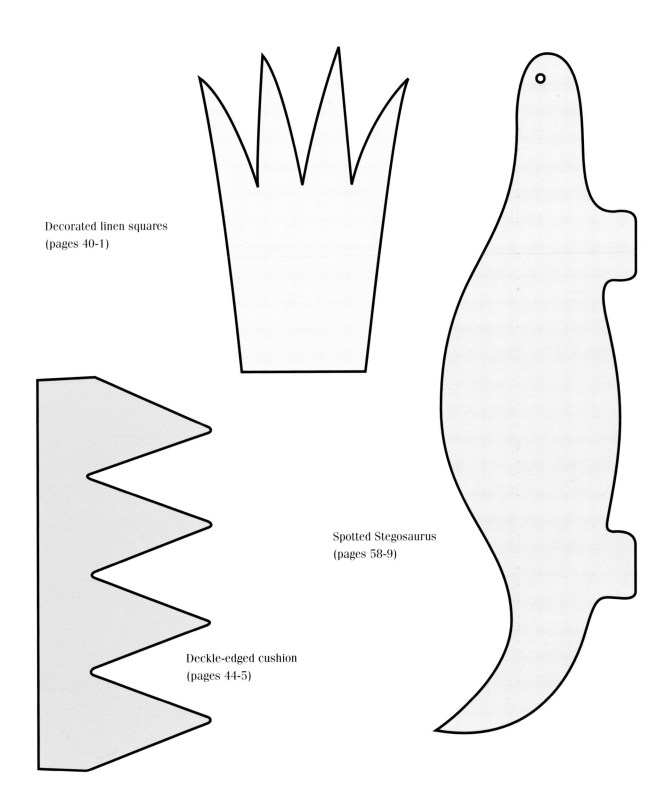

Decorated linen squares
(pages 40-1)

Deckle-edged cushion
(pages 44-5)

Spotted Stegosaurus
(pages 58-9)

Bean bag frog
(pages 54-5)

Appliqué peapod
(pages 38-9)

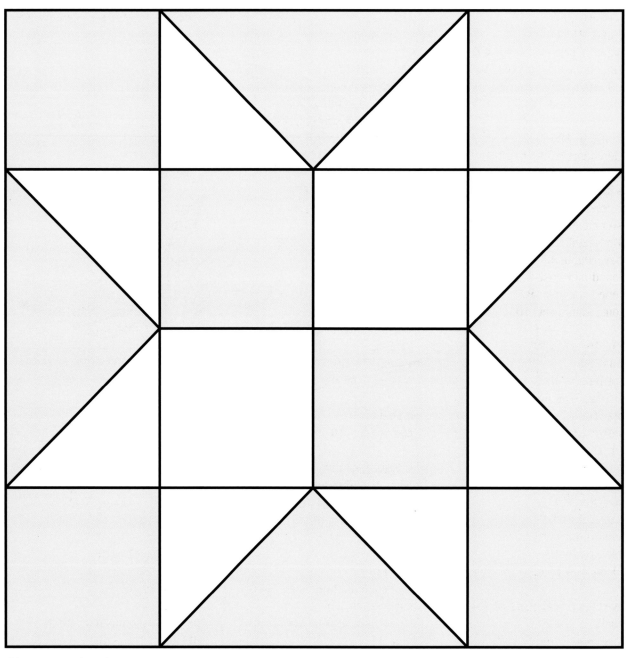

Ohio star patchwork
(pages 50-1)

# Index